PLAIN TALK about FINE WINE

Justin Meyer

PLAIN TALK
about
FINE WINE

Justin Meyer

WITH AN INTRODUCTION
BY ROBERT MONDAVI

CAPRA PRESS
Santa Barbara
1989

To Harold P. Olmo, Ph.D.,
and Brother Timothy, F.S.C., my mentors.

Cover design from an original hand-pulled intaglio print
by etcher Gina Gigli and printer Ruggero Gigli of Villa Gigli Press
Author photo by Faith Echtermeyer
Cover layout by Francine Rudesill
Illustrations by David Jay Flood/A.I.A.
Book design and typography by Jim Cook/Santa Barbara

LIBRARY OF CONGRESS CATALOGING-IN-PUBLICATION DATA
Meyer, Justin, 1938-
    Plain talk about fine wine / Justin Meyer;
with an introduction by Robert Mondavi.
        p.   c.m.
    ISBN 0-88496-300-4: $9.95
    1. Wine and wine making.   I. Title.
TP548.M52   1989
663'.2 — dc20   89-9995 CIP

Published by Capra Press
Post Office Box 2068
Santa Barbara, California 93120

CONTENTS

FOREWORD

By Robert Mondavi

Justin Meyer has written a book which should make all winegrowers proud. This book is accurate, enthusiastic, and fun! Although wine people all have their points of view, Justin and I agree about many, many things. He's allowed me to discuss my feelings concerning the intelligent use of wine, and here they are.

At the Robert Mondavi Winery, we view wine as an integral part of our culture, heritage, and the gracious way of life.

We believe wine is the temperate, civilized, sacred, romantic mealtime beverage recommended in the Bible. It is a liquid food that has been part of civilization for 8,000 years. Wine has been praised for centuries by statesmen, scholars, poets, and philosophers. It has been used as a religious sacrament, as the primary beverage of choice for food, and as a source of pleasure and diversion.

Wine is the natural beverage for every celebration: the birth of a child, graduations, engagements, weddings, anniversaries, promotions, family gatherings, toasts between governments, and other festivities.

There is a growing situation, however, which I believe is of great importance to all of us who enjoy wine—it is something that concerns me deeply. For the past five years, the neo-prohibitionists and anti-alcohol people have stated repeatedly that wine is a hazard and is dangerous to our way of life. This is not the truth—nowhere near the whole truth. These groups talk only of the abuse of wine— not its many benefits. When wine is drunk moderately and intelligently, it is part of gracious living. Abuse wine and just like many other things in our culture—food and medicine among them—it is bad for you.

As a result, the Robert Mondavi Winery has conducted nearly three years of research on the history of wine and we have launched an educational campaign, the Mission, to tell the full story about wine—the benefits and detriments. The program includes symposiums featuring experts in topics ranging from medicine and biology to sociology and religion to deliver the truth about wine and its proper use as a mealtime beverage of moderation.

Common sense tells me wine has been with us since civilization began and will be with us indefinitely. Now, it is up to us to educate ourselves and the American public about what wine really is. In other nations, the products of agriculture, wine included, form an integral part of the country's positive programs. But in America, the promotion of wine, food, music, and art is primarily the responsibility of the private sector—there is very little done by the government to subsidize public relations activities.

During the past 22 years, we have had a wine revolution in California and our wines are now recognized as belonging in the company of fine wines of the world. We will be the shining light in wine for the next several generations. We must tell this story loudly and clearly to our own people and the world at large.

I call this work a mission for all of us involved in the world of wine as producers, consumers, or members of the wine trade. Like Justin, we're pledged to communicate about wine, and his books helps us all.

ACKNOWLEDGEMENTS

You will find no footnotes or bibliography in PLAIN TALK. I have quoted freely, sometimes verbatim, from many sources.

I would like to acknowledge the people from whom I gleaned much of my material—my professors at the University of California at Davis: Professors Min Akiyoshi, Maynard Amerine, Hod Berg, Jim Cook, Jim Guymon, Ralph Kunkee, Lloyd Lider, Klayton Nelson, C. S. Ough, Vern Singleton, and Dinny Webb. I never had the opportunity of studying under Professor Albert Winkler, but his book, General Viticulture, has been and continues to be the "bible" for all of us who pursue that subject.

Wine and Your Well Being by Salvatore Lucia, M.D. provided much of my early knowledge about the health aspects of wine. More recently the Wine Institute and the Winegrowers of California have published two excellent booklets entitled "Wine and America" from which I have drawn for the chapters "Wine and Your Health" and "Wine Use in the United States."

A special thanks goes to Dr. Harold Olmo, under whom I did my master's work; I had the opportunity to live with him and his wife, Helen, for two years. There I learned as much about grape growing during dinner table conversations as I did in the classroom. (From Helen Olmo I also learned the key to culinary success: stall dinner until all the guests are well marinated).

Brother Timothy, Cellarmaster of the Christian Brothers winery, was "patient enough to deal with me as I came out of the university, intolerably smart and ready to conquer the wine world." He taught me to blend my newfound technology with the art of winecrafting.

If any of these sources honor me by reading this book, or parts of it, they may come across statements which sound surprisingly like their own words. I prefer not to be guilty of plagiarism, but if some parts appear to be verbatim, remember, there was a time when plagiarism was seen as the highest form of flattery among writers.

JUSTIN MEYER, *Winegrower*
Silver Oak Cellars
Oakville, California

*The key to wine enjoyment
is having confidence in
your own choices.*

INTRODUCTION

Why "Plain Talk"?

About three years ago a good friend of mine dropped out of the Napa Valley Vintners Association because he thought it had gotten too serious, too political. All he wanted to do at the monthly meetings was eat, drink and have a good time.

While I remained in the Vintners Association he and I created a new organization for the exclusive purpose of eating, drinking and frolicking. To make sure this group was accorded proper respect we named it the "Gastronomical Order for Nonsensical and Dissipatory Segregation." We then invited vintners from ten of Napa Valley's finest wineries to join us for a monthly lunch, each of us hosting once a year. Lunch sometimes goes on until 7 P.M. I usually learn more about what's going on in the valley during that lunch than I do the rest of the month.

We even boast a club car, an unrestored, dirt-brown 1947 airport limo, the longest thing you have ever seen. In it we're ferried to and from our gatherings.

There may be as much wine knowledge assembled at these get-togethers as anywhere in the world. But rarely do you hear descriptions about the "body, legs or audacity" of the wines on the table. To these guys wine is a staple! You can tell when one of these well-known vintners is truly impressed—he'll stand up and say "This is a damned nice wine. I wish I'd made it."

All of these vintners understand that wine production is a continuous, natural process that begins with planting the vine and goes on until the cork is pulled for drinking. If any step of the process is neglected or omitted, the product suffers. Therefore, this book does more than talk about drinking wine. It will address the entire process of wine production, from the vine itself to growing, crushing, fermentation and aging.

I wish my old dad would've had the foresight to leave me independently wealthy. Being a railroad laborer he didn't have much to leave. Since I have to work for a living, I can't think of too many other things I'd rather be than a winegrower. I really enjoy my work. Wine has become my interest and my hobby. I look forward to going to work every day. I also look forward to a glass of wine and dinner with family and friends. Being a winegrower adds a dimension to that pleasure.

I sometimes wish I'd become as interested in a hobby or a game as I am in wine. I've met people who can't wait for the weekends to do what they really enjoy. While I do enjoy racquetball, bike riding, and fishing, it rarely occurs to me that I'd rather skip work and do one of the above. My life has been anything but dull. Fifteen years as a monk (a Christian Brother) and almost twenty-five years in the wine business, a marriage and a family have helped make my first half century rewarding.

I assume that this book attracted your attention because you share my enthusiasm for wine. I want you to be as comfortable as I am with vino and with your choice of it.

When you hear the word wine, I hope it conjures up happy memories— maybe of a wonderful visit to the wine country, or of a great meal when the food and drink perfectly complemented each other; or maybe it was just a nice bottle of wine with a very special friend at a picnic.

Unfortunately, the subject might make some of you uneasy because of an unpleasant experience you've had. I'm certain there have been times when many of us have felt unsure about which wine to select

11

from a restaurant list or which wine to take home for a special dinner. Or how about the wine steward, or maitre d' who, after ridiculing your choice, condescendingly tells you what you really should have selected for that particular dish. Then there's that review you read that called your favorite wine "thin, lacking appeal, and, in short, detestable." Hopefully, these kinds of experiences and our resultant uncertainties haven't prevented us from choosing a wine to enhance our meal.

One thing I hope you'll learn in this book is that wine is really quite simple. It is a food to be enjoyed! Like art or music, the more you know about it, the more you can enjoy it, but you certainly don't need to know any five-syllable words for that.

I sometimes think that the wine cognoscenti, gurus, and snobs, have harmed the cause of vino as much as they have helped it. They speak a language that intimidates and confuses people, giving the impression that only a select minority can genuinely appreciate good wine. To them, I offer the wisdom of Lord Duff Cooper, who said: "There are two reasons for drinking wine: when you are not thirsty— to prevent it; when you are thirsty—to cure it; prevention is always better than cure."

I hope that PLAIN TALK will make you as comfortable with the "fruit of the vine" as you are with food, so that you will be able to select wines with confidence and enjoy them even more. That's not as easy as it sounds because here in America we have no tradition of including wine in the daily meal. When I go to dinner with a group of friends, no one ever asks me to order their food. Frequently, however, the wine list is passed to me. It's true that I might be qualified to decide which is the best wine for the price, but some of my friends might not enjoy that choice any more than they would enjoy filet mignon if they were vegetarians. In the final analysis then, wine, like any food, is a matter of preference and taste. I have attempted to be simple and straightforward in order to help you understand better what you may already know about the subject. I also want to introduce some new and interesting information that will increase your appreciation of it.

For the past several years I have received, on a regular basis, voluminous questionnaires from prospective authors seeking material for books they want to write. I decided that the time had come for a professional winegrower give his view of the wine world.

I refer to myself as a "winegrower" because I have always been involved in the entire process, from the planting of the grapes to the bottling of the finished product. I dislike the term "winemaker" because to me it conjures up an image of manufacturing a product from various ingredients, whereas wine is a natural product. The fact that wine is a natural product is one of several factors which distinguishes it from other alcoholic beverages such as beer and hard liquor. More about that later. For now, suffice to say there are some genuine differences.

As a winegrower, I've had numerous occasions over the years to talk to people about wine. I've traveled around the country promoting my products and I've taught college courses in Wine Appreciation. I've also consumed plenty of wine along the way! In any case, it's long been obvious to me there is a tremendous interest in wine. And the same questions keep coming up. I hope that PLAIN TALK will answer most of them.

As a teacher looking for a classroom text, I never found a book that presented the material quite the way I would have liked. First of all, it seemed to me that in a wine book a brief history is important in order to set the stage. Many texts lacked factual information on viticulture or grape growing. That's an important omission because no vintner on earth can produce a high quality wine from low quality grapes.

To help you understand why some grapes are better than others, a discussion of the importance of climates, soils, grape varieties, cultural practices, and even vine biochemistry is necessary. I want to show you how all these things must come together to produce fine grapes and, ultimately, fine wine.

Chapters 5 through 10 are technical, but don't be intimidated. They will give you solid information on the production of quality grapes and wine, which in turn should give you greater confidence in your choices. There are several ways to approach this book, but remember—a glass of wine in your hand will help what you're reading make a lot more sense.

You will see that my wine world is in the United States, primarily California. The focus is on California because it produces more than

90 percent of all the wine made in America. I'll use two regions, the Napa and Alexander Valleys, plus one variety, Cabernet Sauvignon, in many of my examples because they are what I know best. I wish to acknowledge the many outstanding varieties of wine being produced in other regions of California and in other states. References to foreign wines will be minimal. I have absolutely no desire to promote foreign wines.

Use this book to increase your knowledge and confidence. And enjoyment. If you come to trust your own judgment, I consider the book a success.

There are, of course, objective standards for judging whether a wine is properly made and technically correct. But very few made in California or the United States these days have obvious technical flaws. (For this, we can thank the schools of enology and viticulture at the University of California, Davis and Cal State University, Fresno).

Your subjective judgment of wine is useful and important! After all, your personal reactions are what make wine-tasting fun. Remember, then, that you are your own expert. This book and others, plus reviewers' opinions of wine, may serve as guides. But don't be intimidated if your preferences are different from mine or someone else's. Trust your palate—it is your truth.

"Okay, so it has sophisticated assertiveness, presumptuous breeding, crisp authority, complex balance, elegant power, and respected finesse: What's it taste like?"
—ANONYMOUS

I.

Wine Tasting and Appreciation

You don't have to know much about wine to enjoy it—let me say this loud and clear. The great thing about food and wine is that everyone is right. We all have the basic equipment for enjoyment—the senses of sight, smell and taste. I encourage you to enjoy what you like and reiterate what I said earlier: Have confidence in your own choices.

Yet as with art, music and food, the more you know about wine, the more you can appreciate it. Appreciation can be defined as "a discriminating enjoyment." Thus, the more knowledge we have about the subject, the more we can discriminate and our appreciation can reach a higher level. The consumer, the critic, and the vintner all have varying degrees of appreciation for the same vintage. They may taste the wine at different stages of its maturity and they may taste it for different reasons. The reasons may be pure pleasure or the requirements of their professions; nonetheless, they all appreciate the wine.

Evaluation is somewhat different than appreciation, because in order to evaluate, you determine the worth of an object. This requires more skills, training and background, and yet we find that many qualified tasters appraise wines quite differently. So we must talk about the objective and the subjective realities of evaluation. How subjective? I once led a tasting where I complained emphatically about a certain wine. Rated it dead last. All the while my wife who was seated to my left tugged at my coat whispering "I think it's ours." What does she know? Sure enough, she was right. Luckily, the group liked it, thought I must have been joking. I blamed it on my sinuses. No wonder vintners mince words when asked to lead a blind tasting.

Let's begin by discussing the ideal conditions for tasting. These are the kind of conditions that researchers at the universities require so that the evaluation has scientific and statistical significance. Few of us will ever be in this position, but as we go along I'll try to make it more applicable to our own situation.

First, we should be in a relaxed, comfortable atmosphere, with an appropriate physical environment, including the lack of odors and distractions. The wine glass is important and I think here it should be just as important to the consumer as it is to the critic, the vintner or the scientist. The container should be clear so that color and clarity can be properly ascertained. It should be a proper size. In many winery tasting rooms, restaurants and homes, you might commonly find a nine to twelve-ounce sampler. Personally, I prefer a twenty to twenty-nine-ounce vessel. Of course, these are ackward in the washing machine, and my wife frequently makes me wash them by hand. If you fill the glass to one-fourth of its capacity and swirl the wine, the aromas and bouquet will fill the headspace giving you the opportunity to put your nose down into it so that you can fully evaluate the smells.

It goes without saying that the container should be clean. I always smell the empty vessel before I put wine into it because frequently it will retain the odor of the soap used in the dishwasher, or it will pick up the aroma of the shelf it was sitting upside down on, or the smell of the cardboard box in which it was packed.

When I'm making blends, or am being serious about my tastings, I pour a small amount of wine into the glass, swirl it thoroughly, dump the wine, smell the empty container to make sure only the wine's aroma prevails, and then pour in more of the wine I am serious about evaluating.

The temperature of the sample is important because the colder it is, the less likely you are to experience all of the aroma and bouquet, which simply will not come out under cold conditions. By the same token, a wine sample which is too warm may have lost these aromas and bouquets before you have a chance to evaluate it. Ideally, white wine should be tasted at between 55 and 60 degrees Fahrenheit, while red wine should be tasted at about 5 degrees warmer.

The number of wines you taste is important but this depends on the types. I believe that whites are the easiest to evaluate, reds become more difficult and tire your palate sooner, while dessert types with high sugar or higher alcohol are the most difficult. We find in our own monthly tastings for friends and employees, that six to eight wines is enough. To give the tasters adequate time to evaluate and to discuss those samples takes an hour or more, depending on the group's ability. Those of us who taste regularly together rate wines more consistently and talk about them better, using the same vocabulary. (More about vocabulary of aromas and flavors in a little bit.)

I suggest that you sample by common categories. If you have to mix various types in a tasting, I advise that you go from low-to-high alcohol, from low-to-high sugar, from whites to reds, and finally to dessert types.

When tasting critically, if I use anything to cleanse my palate, it's usually warm water or saltless crackers. But when the sampling is more recreational, I prefer to have some kind of food along with the wine. After all, wine was made to accompany food and to make it more enjoyable. I certainly think that all wines show better next to food. Of course, if the foods are heavily spiced with something like curry or garlic, they will distort your ability to properly evaluate the sample, but there is nothing I like better with a nice glass of red than lamb with plenty of curry or pasta with plenty of garlic.

COLOR

Let's talk about how we use sight, smell and taste in evaluating wine. While smell is the most important of the senses, because it is involved in 60 to 70 percent of the appreciation, taste should be the final and ultimate evaluation, because unless we are professional tasters, what we're really interested in is smelling and ultimately drinking the wine.

As mentioned, we generally don't fill the glass more than one-quarter full. By holding it up to natural light (and I stress natural because we cannot properly evaluate the color under artificial light), we can check clarity. The wine may vary from brilliant to dull to cloudy. What might each of the above indicate to us? Naturally, we would like brilliance of clarity. I don't mind a little dull color, because it might indicate to me that the vintner did not overwork or overfilter the wine at the cost of removing character from it.

On the other hand, if a wine is very cloudy, it might indicate some microbiological problem which would be accompanied by undesirable smells and flavors. If a wine is less than brilliant, or has a small amount of sediment in it, it does not mean it is faulty or unacceptable. We should make those ultimate judgments based on smell and taste. With regard to color, we would expect no browning in whites. A slight amount of green or gold is common. Dessert whites, such as a late-harvest Riesling, with natural sugar present, frequently have a gold hue. Reds may vary from ruby red in their youth, to brick red as they progress, and finally take on a tawny tone in their older age. All of these are acceptable and, in fact, the trained taster may be able to tell something about the age of a red by detecting the various colors described.

AROMA

The sense of smell is extremely important. There are probably at least ten thousand odors which we can detect by the olfactory sense. I might here define a few terms. Threshold is the minimum detectable concentration of a constituent which can be identified. Aroma and bouquet are frequently misunderstood or used incorrectly even by knowledgeable tasters. Here's the way I try to keep them separate in my own mind. I think of varietal aroma, since it is the smell of the grape or grape variety, such as recognizing the aroma of Cabernet Sauvignon (of course, describing that aroma is a whole different matter). Bouquet is developed by the processing or aging odors, such as oak, bottle bouquet, the nuttiness of a sherry, or any other odor that the wine has picked up during processing, bottling, etc., that is distinctive from the varietal aroma. Under the category of desirable smells, we might include such words as vinous, berry, varietal, nutty, and oakey.

The amount of oak extracted during aging will evoke different reactions from different tasters. Many people love a heavily-oaked wine. In my opinion, oak should complement the wine but be subtle enough so that it cannot be identified as oak. I believe it was one of my professors, Dr. Maynard Amerine, who told our class that once you can identify oak as such, it has become a defect.

I find some of these very toasty-oak Chardonnays hard to accept. I tell people that if I wanted that much oak, I would simply drink the Chardonnay and chew on a toothpick. I realize this is a subjective judgment and that is why I look for Chardonnays whose varietal characteristics are outstanding and the oak only a complement. Others sing high praise of these very toasted-oak whites.

Undesirable odors might, for example, be moldy, corky, rubbery, hot, rotten eggs (hydrogen sulfide) or vinegary. These all have something to do with processing, or lack of processing, and so would come under the category of bouquet. No vintner is flattered to see the above words used to describe his wines. I mentioned the words moldy and corky. I believe that the biggest single quality control problem in wine production today is the cork. Cork comes from the bark of a cork oak tree, most of the world supply being grown in Spain, Portugal or thereabouts. As there is more demand for a limited resource we find it more difficult to obtain a consistent high quality source. I believe a great percentage of defective bottled wines are the result of a moldy or corky character caused by faulty corks.

cork tree
gotcha!

TASTE

We recognize only four basic tastes: sweet as in sugar, sour as in acid, bitter as in quinine, and salty. If you saw your tongue under a microscope, it would appear to contain approximately 50,000 small cups. Each of these cups is a taste bud. We have a different type of taste bud for each of the four tastes. Primarily, the buds for sweet are at the front of the tongue. Behind that and along the sides are the salty receptors. Then come the sour perceivers, and, on the back of the tongue, the taste buds for bitterness. When we are tasting it is necessary to develop certain techniques of moving the wine around in the mouth in order to make sure we are experiencing all four tastes. Otherwise, we might not encounter all the flavors in the wines. The best and most obvious example is when we hear the term "bitter aftertaste." Because we did not move the wine around in our mouth, we only experienced the bitter when we finally swallowed the wine and it went over the back of our tongue. Had we simply tasted the wine without moving it around on our tongue, then spitting it out, we might not have had the entire experience. It can be quite amusing to watch adept tasters chew and slurp their wines using their various favorite techniques to move the sample around in their mouth.

Some examples of desirable tastes are fruit, acid, and sugar, while undesirable might be considered too flat or too tart, too sweet or too bitter. I should point out, though, that tannin (the astringency or puckeriness of a red wine) is experienced by the sense of touch rather than by the sense of taste. You will hear people mistakenly refer to puckeriness as a taste. Tannin actually gets into your taste buds and grabs you, thus causing the puckeriness. What happens to reds when they age is that tannin molecules link up with an oxygen bond, forming chains so long that eventually they no longer fit into the cup-shaped taste bud and thus the wine tastes smoother.

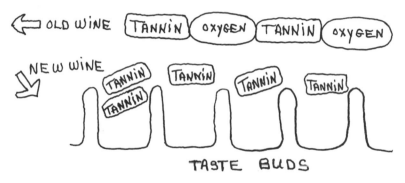

"Body" is a term frequently used for descriptive purposes while tasting. Body probably means more things to more people than any other term employed by tasters. It's a complex concept referring to viscosity or weight in wine. It is related to the alcohol content and usually is the opposite of thinness or wateriness, but body can also be affected by diacetyl which is a natural product of fermentation, or by vanillin which can be an extract of oak barrels. "Finish" is another word used to describe wines and usually refers to the end of the taste.

What about distinguishing wine characteristics? I think we have to separate the objective from the subjective. The objective reality might be that a "wine has character" or "the wine has a particular defect." As I participate in promotional tastings around the country where 30 or more wineries are represented in a given room, it occurs to me that there are fewer and fewer wines made with noticeable defects. Thus it gets down to why I like one better than another. When someone does say that one wine is superior to another, my reaction is, "Says who?"

The same thing applies when someone says that one is too high-priced. Says who? If I say a product is priced too high, it says more about my budget than the drink. I think critics have to be extremely careful when they comment on the prices of wines. They are telling us more about their economic situation than they are about the wine. If I own an elegant sports car, you would be wasting your time to tell me that your compact at one-third the price is just as good.

I have to laugh when I see a rating system in a wine publication which gives a $6.00 Chardonnay a 94 out of 100 points and a $20.00 Chardonnay a 78. Oh, sure, the $6.00 Chardonnay could be better but if that's true, both producers should re-examine their pricing policies.

When I read reviews, I am curious about the taster's or the panel's comments. But I'm a big enough boy to judge for myself whether I want to pay that price for the wine or not. What I don't need is a consumer champion trying to ingratiate himself with consumers by making quality/price decisions. I think that whenever rating systems do this, they lose their objectivity. Let's face it, there are some people who prefer to pay more for a product. The value of the critic is to report which product is the best. If the critics and the panels would stick to the objective judging of wines, there would be more uniformity among their results.

One day I read a favorable review of a certain wine. The next day I saw that the same one ranked in the middle or the end of another reviewer's results. I had to shake my head. Did something happen to the wine? Not likely. One review was faulty and more times than not the fault is connected with the subjective rather than with the objective part of the judgment.

The last wine I ever entered in a competition was our 1978 vintage which I thought was one of the best we ever made. At its best, it won a gold medal and the sweepstakes award as best of show. It also garnered a gold and a silver in two other competitions. How about the two competitions where it was a "no show"? I don't believe the wine changed. I know the panels were different and I believe that when you taste 100 entries in a day, it's very difficult to do a good job. So the bottom line of this for the consumer is that if you have a critic or a retailer who has consistently recommended wines which, when you tasted them, you enjoyed, continue to follow their advice. On the other hand, if something you happen to like receives bad reviews, don't be intimidated. You're paying the tab so you are your own best expert.

OTHER METHODS OF TASTING

If you want to do some serious tasting, either by yourself or with a group, you might consider scorecards or rating systems and you surely want to taste "blind." By this, I mean brown-bagging the bottles, or in some fashion eliminating the influence of the label and the price on your decision. One helpful training exercise would be to set up solution tastings. The easiest way to do this is to buy a "simple" white wine (I say simple because a wine with less character will have less likelihood of masking the features you are trying to identify). Put this white wine in four glasses: keep one as it is for the control, and to the next three add incremental amounts of something like citric acid (lemon juice), tannic acid, or any other smell or flavor components you would like to educate your palate about, such as sugar, mint, blackberry, apple, eucalyptus, olive, mushroom, cardboard, vinegar, oak chips, chocolate, or any other things you see used in wine descriptions. In this way you can acquaint yourself with these features when you run across them.

Another simple, interesting experiment, is to use a black glass so that you cannot see the color of the wine when you taste it or taste blindfolded. Smell and taste the wine and see how not being able to determine the color influences your judgment before you smell and taste.

Good objective ratings are the paired test and the triangular test. In the paired test, you are repeatedly given the same two wines in two different glasses to see if you can accurately and consistently tell them apart. In the triangular test you would have the same wine in two

SCORECARD
TWENTY POINT TASTING SYSTEM

		A	B
APPEARANCE 0-2			
CLOUDY 0			
CLEAR 1			
BRILLIANT 2			
COLOR 0-2			
DISTINCTLY OFF (FOR TYPE) 0			
SLIGHTLY OFF 1			
CORRECT 2			
AROMA AND BOUQUET 0-4			
FAINT 1			
SLIGHT 2			
PRONOUNCED 3			
SUBTRACT 1 OR 2 FOR OFF-ODORS			
ADD 1 FOR NOTICEABLE BOUQUET FROM AGING			
ACETIC ACID (VINEGARY) 0-2			
OBVIOUS 0			
SLIGHT 1			
NONE 2			
TOTAL ACID 0-2			
DISTINCTLY LOW OR HIGH FOR TYPE 0			
SLIGHTLY LOW OR HIGH 1			
NORMAL 2			
SWEETNESS 0-1			
TOO HIGH OR LOW FOR TYPE 0			
NORMAL 1			
BODY 0-1			
TOO HIGH OR LOW FOR TYPE 0			
NORMAL 1			
FLAVOR 0-2			
DISTINCTLY ABNORMAL OR DEFICIENT 0			
SLIGHTLY ABNORMAL 1			
NORMAL 2			
ASTRINGENCY 0-2			
DISTINCTLY HIGH FOR TYPE 0			
SLIGHTLY HIGH 1			
NORMAL 2			
GENERAL QUALITY 0-2			
LACKING 0			
SLIGHT 1			
IMPRESSIVE 2			
TOTAL*			

* U.S. WINES ALMOST ALWAYS SCORE 13 OR MORE

glasses with a different wine in the third to see if you can identify the odd sample. Subjective rating systems would be the scorecard, and you see this done on 20 point or 100 point totals, the use of a ranking system, or simply a preference test. I think scorecards are useful when you are a beginning taster because they have various categories such as body, astringency, acidity, overall quality, and so on, that you are forced to judge separately, thus training you to identify these characteristics. The more I taste, the less I like to use a scorecard system. If forced to, I will give the wine a bottom line score that makes some sense from my experience and then back into the various categories to deduct points from the total. In our own company tastings that we have for fun and to educate our employees, we use a ranking system, as I believe it is less intimidating. All you're saying is, I prefer wine X as my top choice of six wines and below it rank the rest to my least-favorite choice. With each wine we try to use some descriptive terms of sight, smell or taste to force ourselves to identify why we liked or disliked it.

After years of participating in various kinds of tastings, I have come to the conclusion that there are "tasting wines" and there are "drinking wines." Tasting wines might be those with some strong characteristic that gets your attention and, therefore, you rate it high. After the tasting is over, I always like to leave the bottles out on the bar and see which one gets drunk first. To me that is the winner. I find some people might rate a wine very high in the tasting but find after the second glass that, for some reason, they simply don't want any more.

As I grow older and have tasted more, I find that I put a much higher premium on subtlety and complexity than on forwardness or aggressiveness in a wine. I think one thing we should all be aware of is that Americans have a sweet tooth. We were raised on chocolate bars and soft drinks and if you look at the wines which created the big stir over the years, they have been cold duck, pop wines, coolers, and blush wines. All of these are generally a little sweet and easy to drink. Americans typically start out liking slightly sweet wines and if they ever progress onward, they go to drier white wines, then to fruity light-bodied reds, such as a Beaujolais, and it might be ten years before they can enjoy a good full-bodied Zinfandel or Cabernet

Sauvignon. So we have a ladder or progression in wine appreciation and if we try to make someone jump three rungs of that ladder, he's liable to fall flat on his face.

A typical winery tasting-room conversation might go something like this. "Sir, would you like a dry wine or a slightly sweet wine?" Now, Americans have correlated "sweet wine" with Muscatel and "wino" so they ask for a dry wine. When you give them a nice dry wine, they say, "That's sour; do you have anything less sour?" So you give them a slightly sweet wine and they say, "That's a nice dry wine." So, as the man said in the movie *Cool Hand Luke,* "What we have here is a failure to communicate."

Have you noticed that since sweet is a bad word, some people have started using in its place the term "fruity"? I think this is a terrible term because even though I like my fruit sweet, I don't consider sweet necessarily fruity. But I think we have to recognize where the American palate is coming from, lest we run the risk of offering them at the beginning a good dry wine and they decide they don't like wine at all. What they really meant is that they don't like this wine! Unfortunately, they may never try a glass of wine again.

VOCABULARY

On to vocabulary and wine tasting. The question posed in a recent article was, "Why do people talk about wine?" The answers: one, to communicate information for some pragmatic purpose; two, to show off one's knowledge; three, to put down the listener. But did you ever stop to consider that there is no vocabulary for taste and smell and that people do not apply words to things in the same way? What did the man mean when he said that "This wine is soft but I would say that it is graceful rather than sensuous"? And how about the famous caption by James Thurber in the *New Yorker* cartoon—"It's a naive, domestic Burgundy without much breeding, but I think you'll be amused by its presumption"? Or the fellow who, after reading a panel's evaluation of Cabernet Sauvignons, wrote:

> I now know how to make the perfect Cabernet. One part water, 30 parts ethanol (industrial grade), 100 parts per

26

million free sulphur dioxide, red dye No. 2 to suit, one part toast-burnt, one part bell pepper and/or fresh jalapeno, dash of vinegar, one chocolate bar and one apricot (for the cognoscenti). Mix ingredients, strain and serve very cold.

DAVIS AROMA WHEEL

In our efforts tò make up for lack of vocabulary which properly describes smells and tastes, we sometimes get carried away. When I'm talking about excellent body, fantastic legs, soft and sensuous appeal, you can bet I'm not talking about a wine.

In the last few years, efforts have been made to help us describe the aroma and structure of wine. The so-called Davis wine aroma wheel, developed by Dr. Ann Noble and associates at U.C. Davis, is included here to help you. At the inner circle, we see that we have terms such as fruity, spicy, woody, earthy and vegetative, commonly used to describe characteristics of wine. Let's take fruity as an example. In the middle concentric ring, this is developed further into citrus, berry, tree fruit, tropical fruit, estery, dried fruit and labrusca, which is a species of grape native to the eastern United States, typified by the smell and taste of the Concord. Then, finally, on the outermost concentric circle, we can further define any one term, such as berry, into blackberry, raspberry, strawberry and black currant. Currant is a term commonly associated with Cabernet Sauvignon, whereas raspberry is frequently used to describe the Zinfandel varietal aroma. I would suggest that as you taste the wine, you start with the innermost circle and after you have chosen the words in that circle which best apply to your wine, then move to the outer circle to try to further define what you're smelling and tasting.

Vedel's red wine structure graph is an attempt to integrate the structural features of red wine. The best balanced wine is at the center of the circle, while wines that are unbalanced toward acidity, astringency, or sucrosity (sweetness) are located somewhere beyond the center of the circle.

Wine tasting is a complex experience in which sight, smell, taste and feel are intermingled and one of the things which differentiates

THE AROMA WHEEL
Showing first, second and third tier terms, Noble, et al.
(Copyright: American Society of Enologists and Viticulturists)

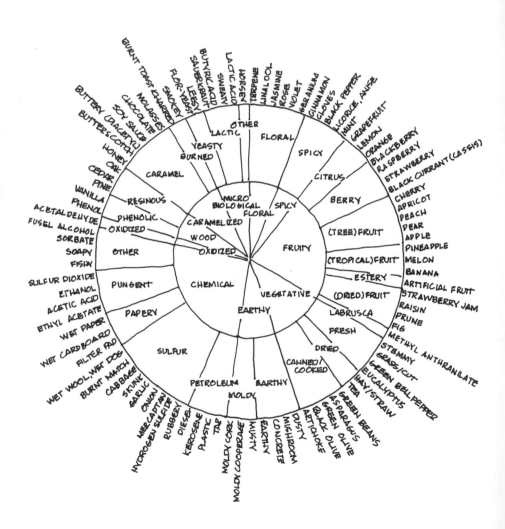

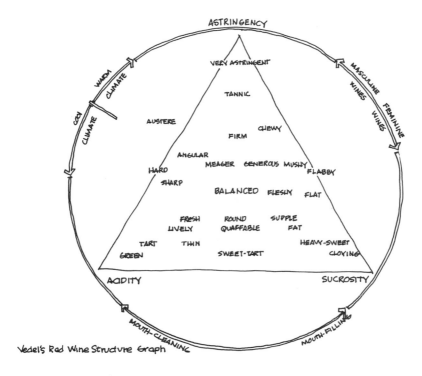

ASTRINGENCY

VERY ASTRINGENT

TANNIC

CHEWY
AUSTERE
FIRM

ANGULAR
MEAGER GENEROUS MUSHY
HARD
FLABBY
SHARP
BALANCED FLESHY FLAT

FRESH ROUND SUPPLE
LIVELY QUAFFABLE FAT

TART THIN HEAVY-SWEET
GREEN CLOYING
SWEET-TART

ACIDITY SUCROSITY

WARM CLIMATE
COOL CLIMATE
MASCULINE WINES
FEMININE WINES

MOUTH-CLEANING
MOUTH-FILLING

Vedel's Red Wine Structure Graph

an expert from the other is the expert's ability to separate and identify these various experiences.

READING A WINE LABEL

Let's move on to reading a wine label, but first let's look at a map that shows the geography of grape growing in California. The Golden State is vast and contains many grape-growing regions with different soil and climatic characteristics. These can have a substantial influence on the character and the quality of the wine. The producer's name and reputation, along with his location and the appellation (the name of the area where the grapes were grown, such as Napa Valley, Sonoma County, Monterey, etc.), all tell you something about the wine. I would immediately expect a Napa or Sonoma Cabernet Sauvignon to be quite different from Monterey's, primarily because of the climatic differences of the regions. That's not to say better or worse, but different. The vintage is the year in which the grapes were grown.

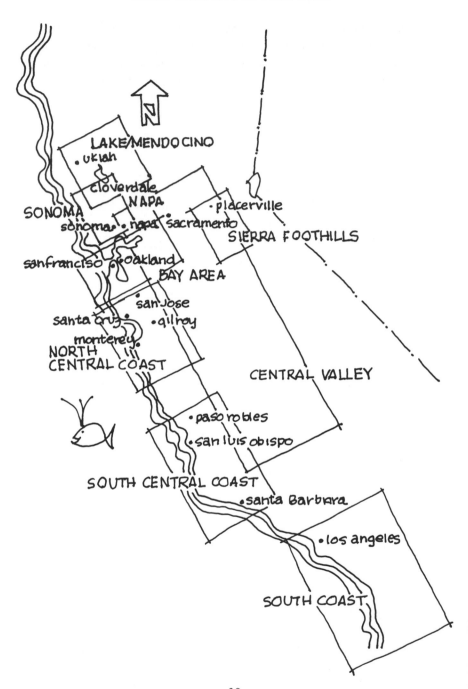

This is important because the weather or growing conditions of that year have an influence on the quality of the wine. The grapes or wine must be 95 percent from that particular year. Because of the growing conditions of rainfall, heat, drought, and so on, we have "good years" and "bad years." I would generalize by saying that in California we have a more even climate than in Europe so while they have great and disastrous years, we have generally been able to avoid the bottom end of the scale, but that is not to say that "every year is a vintage year in California," as was once proclaimed.

The name of the wine is also on the label. If 75 percent of it is from one type of grape, such as Chardonnay or Chenin Blanc, Pinot Noir or Zinfandel, the name of that variety will appear on the bottle. If it does not satisfy the 75 percent requirement, it may be called red table wine, white table wine: many people still use the term Burgundy or Chablis for table wines, which peeves the French no end.

There are other terms such as "estate bottled," "produced and bottled by," "cellared and bottled by," but to me these are of lesser importance. I'm always amazed at the number of people who ask me if I grow my own grapes. The people who sell "estate bottled wines" generally proclaim that their wines are superior because they grew their own grapes. Again we cannot generalize. It's rather egotistical to think that you can grow grapes better than the other fellow and too many times I have seen independent growers bring in beautiful sound fruit only to be criticized by the vintner because there are a few leaves in the gondola. Then rolls in the next gondola, the grapes are full of mildew and rot, which is a much more serious problem, but they are acceptable because they are winery or estate grown.

The French, who have been growing grapes centuries longer than we in California, have come to recognize that Chateau X, for instance, with its own unique combination of soil, climate and varieties, produces a wine which can be identified in a blind tasting by afficionados of that Chateau. The grapes come year after year from that one property, are taken to the cellar on the property, and made into wine. Thus, their term "mis en bouteilles au chateau" has a more significant meaning for them than "estate bottled" or "produced and bottled by" on a California label. As the California wine industry develops more history and the supply of grapes to a particular winery becomes more consistent, terms such as "estate bottled" and "produced and bottled by" will have more meaning.

To give you a good example, at one time I owned and was the vintner at two separate wineries. We chose for economic reasons to crush and ferment all the wine at the larger facility. Even though we owned both facilities and even though I was the vintner for all the wines, we still could only put "produced and bottled by" on one label and "cellared and bottled by" on the other. The logic of the government was that if you do not ferment and bottle the wine at that particular facility, you cannot say that you "produced it" but only "made" or "cellared" the wine.

You have to understand that I'm talking about California or American labels. When you're reading the European label, it might be quite different and it may even differ from country to country. I had to laugh one time when talking to Dr. Helmut Becker at the Geisenheim Research Station on the Rheingau in Germany. He said there was a problem with the wine laws that governed all of the European Economic Community. The problem was that "the Germans kept them to the letter of the law, the French kept them when it was convenient, and the Italians didn't even know they had been published."

Let's talk about one of my pet peeves for a minute. The U.S. law used to be that to call a wine by the varietal name, such as Cabernet Sauvignon, the wine had to be made 51 percent from that variety. The Government, to satisfy demands from consumer advocates for truth in advertising, pushed the limit up to 75 percent. Does this make the wine any better? Is 100 percent Cabernet better than a blend of 70 percent Cabernet, 20 percent Merlot, 10 percent Cabernet Franc? By our U.S. law standards, most of the products of the great chateaus of Bordeaux, such as Lafitte, Haut Brion, Margaux, Cheval Blanc, Ausone, and Pichon Lalande, could not qualify as varietal wines. In fact, if you read the labels of some of the famous chateaus of Bordeaux, they simply say "red table wine." Why do the gurus and the cognoscenti make such a fuss about the varietal content or percentage in a California wine, then turn around and pay $100 a bottle for a generic red table wine from Bordeaux? I'm not knocking the quality of the foreign products, but only the double standard by which foreign and domestic wines are judged.

PRICES

The same could be said of the prices. If a California or domestic wine gets over $15 or $20, it is "racey" in price. Again, who says? But that same critic who might comment about the $20 California or domestic wine being "racey" doesn't even mention price when evaluating a $100 bottle of foreign wine.

It all gets down to a matter of taste! I truly believe that you like best that to which you are most accustomed. We regularly put a good Bordeaux in our blind tastings along with California Cabernets. Almost every time I can pick out the Bordeaux by smell alone. The most common characteristic is that they have a "cedary, cigar box" odor which I do not find in most California wines. Upon tasting them, I find they are low alcohol, thin-bodied and hard tannin. A Frenchman tasting a California wine might find it "aggressive, alcoholic, high in extract and flabby."

So what does that tell us? The weather conditions in 1982 had been good in Bordeaux. They produced a wine which in aroma, flavor, and mouth feel I found difficult to distinguish from our California Cabernet Sauvignons in our "blind tastings." I think the French were rather disturbed when people started referring to the 1982 Bordeaux' as "California-like." The above may also tell us that taste is a subjective matter which may not be defined by two tasters . . . even trained tasters, in the same way.

Returning to price for a minute, have you ever thought about the following absurdity? How many other industries have been able to convince you that the higher price you have to pay and the longer you have to wait to use the product should be the criteria for excellence and desirability? I cringe when I see the review of a $100 wine when it says it is a "big, hard, closed-in wine which will not be at its peak for 20 years but should be well worth the wait." How many of us are going to be around to enjoy it?

When people ask me, "How long will this wine age?" I want to answer with the question, "How large is your wine cellar?" I think those questions are asked simply to make the questioner look good and knowledgeable, but the reality is that few persons have a cellar large enough to accumulate any quantity of stock to hold the wine for the number of years they are talking about.

So let's get out and try some wines. Try to describe them with the most objective words that mean something to other people. Trust your palate; drink what you enjoy. If you find something you think will age, buy more than one bottle, preferably at least a case, and put it away; then periodically open a bottle and track its development. Try to match it up with various foods to see how the wine comes across differently with each match. But above all, enjoy! If you don't, switch from wine to something more enjoyable — like stamp collecting.

"A meal without wine is like
a day without sunshine."

FRENCH PROVERB

2.

Wine as Food

I recently had the pleasure of lunching with a very classy lady. I'd have to call her elderly because she must've been close to 70, yet she had that twinkle in her eyes that told you she would never grow old. Someone brought up the quote at the head of this chapter and her reply was, "A meal without wine is like making love by yourself."

Used in moderation, wine is good for your health. (See Chapter 3.) I have always viewed wine as food and certainly it fits Webster's definition of "nutritive material taken into the body of an organism for purposes of growth, work or repair and for the maintenance of the vital processes."

Many people survive quite nicely without drinking wine just as there are plenty of people who don't eat peanut butter. So the fact that many people survive without sipping the fruit of the vine doesn't mean that it does not fit Webster's definition. The fact that it's displayed prominently at the dinner table, in restaurants, and in grocery stores (at least in most areas), tells me that most people recognize wine as a food. I attribute the success of my own wine to my having always perceived it as food, and having tried to produce a pleasant beverage that tastes even better at the table. This may seem a rather simple and obvious premise, but over the last 20 years I have seen producers get caught up in esoteric wines that might be "interesting" to taste but not very enjoyable to drink.

Wine definitely has the properties of food. It is nutritious and contains vitamins, calories and other values. Moreover, it is now widely used in hospitals to accompany meals because it relaxes, sharpens the appetite, and makes food more savory.

I would not think of sitting down to dinner without a bottle of wine on the table. I've simply found that after having wine to accompany a fine meal, milk, water and coffee simply don't "do it" anymore. I like the quote from Jonathan Swift: "This wine should be eaten; it is much too good to drink." On the other hand, I rarely indulge in a glass with my lunch since I know I will become so relaxed that I would rather take a siesta than go back to work. In this regard, the Europeans have it figured out a lot better than we do. The big meal is at noon when they might have a few glasses, then take two hours off for a nap, go back to work, work late, have a light supper and go to bed without a lot of food in their stomachs. A wise old monk once told me we should "eat breakfast like a king, eat lunch like a prince and eat supper like a pauper."

STORAGE

The storage conditions for wine, as with other perishables, are critical. Ideally, it should be stored in an area where the temperature is constant between 55 and 60 degrees F. The place should be dark and the bottle should be stored either upside down or on its side so that the cork remains moist.

Let's examine each of these factors more closely. The word "constant" is the key here because changes in temperature can cause movement of the cork. Warm temperatures cause fluids to expand. If it happens to be a beverage with some carbon dioxide in it, that gas might come out of solution and thus put pressure on the cork. Either expanding liquid or additional pressure can cause the cork to push and lose its tight seal, causing leakage or allowing oxygen to enter and spoil the wine. We must also keep in mind that aging is a chemical reaction. As such it is hurried by warmer temperatures and slowed by colder ones. Therefore, if you have inventory which you intend to age for a long time, cooler temperatures are more important. Realistically, most people will drink the wine either the night they buy it or within the first year. Under these conditions 70 degrees F or lower is acceptable.

Light and heat can cause perfectly good vintages to break down. Therefore, a wine stored in the dark is better off than having one stored in either natural or artificial light. Probably the simplest and best storage area in a house without a cellar is a hallway closet. It has no windows and generally is more central to the house so the temperature would be less variable.

AGING

The next common question is, "Under proper conditions, how much age is needed for a wine?" Again, this is a subjective judgment. We can make some generalizations. A white will usually reach its peak, plateau, and then decline in quality more quickly than a red. A large bottle, such as a magnum, double magnum, or imperial (6 liters), will age slower than a 750ml or a so called "fifth." Again, if you were going to drink your wines sooner you would be better off with 750ml bottles because they will age faster and reach maturity sooner. If you wanted to put bottles away for a long time, you might want to choose a larger size. For instance, I generally try to buy magnums or larger for my children's wine cellar because in the larger-size bottle, these wines have a better chance of making it to my kids' twenty-first birthdays.

Earlier I indicated my annoyance at the question, "How long will this wine age?" Maybe I'm over-reacting by wanting to ask, "How large is your wine cellar?" Since the average wine cellar is a 12-bottle rack in the dining room, or a hallway closet with 10 to 15 cases in it, I really doubt that those wines will age long enough to ever reach their peak. Now, if you're a fanatic like myself, and have an 5,000-bottle cellar, you can get into a cycle of drinking 10 to 15 year old wines. Then I believe that the time it takes the item to age is pertinent. Yet again, this is a subjective judgment. For example, if you open a 15-year-old red for a group of dinner guests, some of them will comment

37

that it has many years yet to go, some will think that it's absolutely at its peak, while others might think that it's "over the hill." When I choose wines for aging in my own cellar, flavor and balance are more imporant than whether the wine has a lot of tannin or is a so called "block buster." A mediocre or poorly balanced wine will not achieve balance or improve with age alone.

CHOICE, PRESENTATION AND SERVICE

The key in choosing wine is the food with which it is going to be served. You probably already know the old guidelines for wine/food match-ups. White goes with salad, fish and fowl; red with meats, game and spicy food, and rosé and sparkling wine are acceptable with anything. As you get more confident, you serve whatever you like. My own cellar is probably 90 to 95 percent reds, with the balance being a combination of white, sparkling and dessert wines. I find that people who drink a lot of wine prefer reds, probably because reds are more complex. Since I produce only Cabernet Sauvignon, a red, I am fond of saying that if all wines had their choice, they would be red and that all the great ones of the world are red. But I frequently serve white wine with a salad, fish or fowl, and while you might want to experiment with a Pinot Noir with salmon, or a chilled Zinfandel with fish, I cannot remember any white wines that I particularly like with steak, roast beef or garlic-laced pasta.

The question might arise, "Is food ever subordinate to the wine, rather than choosing the wine to complement the food?" I could think of occasions when you want to pour a very old or otherwise extraordinary wine for a special guest and, thus, choose food that would best show off that selection. But I think it's silly when people gulp down their food without ever commenting on it (and possibly without tasting it) and then swirl and sniff wine, hold it up to the light, and critique it, ad nauseum. I don't advocate gulping down your drink without appreciating it but, rather, that we take the time to appreciate the food as well.

In a restaurant it is good practice that the waiter present the bottle with the cork still intact, and after the guest has assented that it is the wine he indeed ordered, the cork is pulled in the presence of all. This practice probably started so that the unscrupulous would not transfer an inferior vintage into a bottle with a well-known label. The waiter will hand you the cork. This is to give you the opportunity to examine the cork to see that there are no signs of leakage. If you have a particularly snooty waiter and want to have a little fun, give him back the cork and say, "You can have the cork; I'll take the wine."

There are many styles of cork puller. We all know about the corkscrew. One piece of advice: the best are the type that will let you slide a toothpick down the middle of the spiral. If, on the other hand, the corkscrew is solid, like an auger, it may also function like one and simply bore a hole into the middle of the cork, ripping out its center instead of extracting it. I am very fond of the Ah-So, which is a two-pronged cork puller. The prongs fit between the cork and the inside of the bottle neck. Once you learn to use it, it is quicker and easier than a corkscrew and also has the advantage that the cork remains whole and sound should you need to put it back into an unfinished bottle.

One common question I'm asked is, "If you don't finish a bottle, what's the best thing to do?" My answer is, "That's never a problem around our house." Seriously, the best thing to do is put the cork back in and put the wine in the refrigerator. A partial bottle has oxygen in it which will break the wine down. Under refrigeration the oxidative chemical reaction will be slower. Simply bring the bottle, if it happens to be red, out of the refrigerator an hour or so in advance of the meal. I should add that there are times, such as on a hot day, or with certain dishes, like fish, that a chilled red wine tastes good. But please, not "on the rocks," because this will considerably dilute the character of the wine.

There are available now vacuum devices which will extract the air from partially filled bottles before re-corking, or devices which displace the air in the headspace with nitrogen or carbon dioxide. You might want to try one of those. I hear they work quite well.

Much is made of "breathing." I'm not an advocate of letting the wine breathe. Old wines are the wines that have the most need of breathing but if it took 10 to 20 years of bottle age to develop the bouquet, I would like to experience it even if it is a little unpleasant at the beginning. I am confident that if the wine has a little "bottle

39

sickness," a few swirls in the glass will do as much or more than several hours of breathing time. It has not been your imagination if you have thought that a wine has changed in the glass.

To dispel another myth, corks in a bottle do not breathe. Aging in a bottle is an anaerobic process, one that occurs in the absence of oxygen. This is the reason we get a different type of aging in the bottle than we do in the barrel which is aerobic (with oxygen). So "bottle sickness" is generally the result of lack of oxygen or what is called a "reducing reaction" with which "off" odors are associated. As you swirl the wine in your glass and it picks up oxygen, many of the unpleasant odors will disappear in the glass and you may find that it seems to get better as the meal goes on. A very old wine may break down rather quickly in the presence of oxygen. It would be a shame to take a 50 year old wine, let it breathe for five hours before the meal, only to find that the wine has fallen apart during that time. I was pleasantly surprised when I once expressed my opinions concerning breathing in front of a group of vintners and found no opposition. We agreed that the ritual or "breathing" is much overdone.

The glass itself should be clear rather than tinted so that you can examine the color and clarity of the wine. And for heaven's sake, make the glass large enough so that the liquid can be swirled (12 oz. to 29 oz.).

If you would like guidelines for temperatures, here are mine:

Champagne—50° F
Whites, rosés—55° F
Dessert wines—60° F
Reds—65-70° F

As far as I'm concerned, even white and sparkling wines that come out of the cold box are too chilly at 45 degrees F. At such a low temperature you miss many of the aromas and flavors. There is no place in my scheme of things for an ice bucket, even for champagne.

The host takes the first service in order to taste the wine to see if it is acceptable and also so that if a small amount of cork or sediment comes out with the first pour, it doesn't go into the glass of a guest.

COOKING WITH WINE

Let's talk for a moment about cooking with wines. I told you the secret to my culinary art is to stall dinner until the guests are well marinated. Then everything tastes better. I try to use good quality wines in cooking. Very frequently I use the same one for cooking as I will be serving with the dish. Most recipes call for dry wines. This is the other reason for using good quality wines because so many of the lower-price, bulk types are slightly sweet to cover their defects or lack of age. There might be recipes that call for a slightly sweet wine, a sherry or even a vermouth, which is an herb-flavored wine. In fact, if I am cooking a dish that has a lot of herbs in it, I frequently put in a dash of vermouth. I'd be lost in the kitchen without garlic; the secret is to make sure your companion shares the food with you.

The interest in America in gourmet cooking has increased interest in wine as a culinary agent. Wine definitely adds character to food. In fact, for any recipe that calls for the addition of water, you might try adding wine or at least some in the water's place. Using vino in cooking adds few calories since the alcohol evaporates during cooking.

While we're primarily talking about table wines, I might mention that sherry, whites, rosés, blush wines, and even chilled reds are nice as an aperitif. Typical dessert wines are ports, muscats, and "late harvest" types.

WINE IN RESTAURANTS

What about wine in restaurants? Certainly you should not be afraid to request wine in lieu of a cocktail or to have a glass of wine in the bar, and you have the right to expect—even demand—quality wine by the glass. So often in the past, "house wines" have been absolutely terrible. It amazes me that a restaurant that takes pride in the quality of its food and commands high prices will nevertheless serve low-grade house wine just to make sure that their per-glass profit is astronomical. More and more we see the better restaurants offering fine varietal wines (Chardonnay, Cabernet, etc.) of well-known producers by the glass. I think this is a practice to be lauded, encouraged and supported. I know I will commonly order one glass of white wine to have with my salad and then move on to red, and I appreciate it when I have a decent selection.

Let's talk about what makes up a good wine list, both from the restaurant and the customer's point of view. First of all, the wine should be matched to the food's style and complexity. German-style rieslings would be just as out of place in an Italian restaurant as would be hearty, complex reds in a fish house.

The price of the food and wine should be compatible. A family restaurant, specializing in $8 to $12 entrées, is not likely to sell many $30 bottles of wine. The price of the wine should have some reasonable relationship to the price for which the consumer can buy it retail. Some of the most progressive restaurants sell wine at retail plus some reasonable corkage fee. I think this encourages the consumer to drink better wine.

The size of the wine list can vary considerably and still be acceptable. They range from a carefully chosen 20-wine list to award-winning collections. We seem to be seeing less of the telephone-book size wine list. Such a list costs the restaurant a tremendous amount in inventory. From the winery's standpoint, no single wine on such a wine list sells very well. What's more, patrons will become bored and confused trying to read it.

I am astonished at the inadequate storage of many restaurants. Despite the amount of money spent for ambiance, many have closet-sized cellars. It is not uncommon for a lot of restaurants to buy a case at a time. They call the winery in a panic after they have sold their last bottle. I think that as Americans become more knowledgeable about wine, restaurants will find it is worth their while to have a larger cellar so that they can buy adequate stocks of certain vintages; they can begin to accumulate older ones on their list or so-called "vertical tastings" (meaning several different vintages of the same producer and variety of wine). When restaurants have large enough cellars, they are not so apt to be out of items on their list. When I go out to dinner, I make it a practice of patronizing restaurants which carry my wine. It's always disconcerting to find that they are out of it. Part of the blame must be put on our own sales staff. On the other hand, if the wine is selling well and making a good profit for the account, you would think they would not let themselves run out of stock any more than they would exhaust menu items at 8:00 P.M.

Staff training in restaurants is very important. Ideally, the wait staff, or at least the wine steward, should be knowledgeable about every wine on the list. They should be able to answer questions and even make recommendations. It must be very difficult for a waiter to recommend a wine. Knowing the entree that has been ordered and asking what wine you have enjoyed lately, are keys as to which on the list might be most appreciated. I have had waiters "bad mouth" a wine I have ordered in their restaurant. While I think it's legitimate for the waiter to suggest another item on the list, criticizing what you have ordered reflects badly on the customer and on the person who put the list together. . . . most likely his boss!

Can you send a wine back? My answer is that you can send it back for the same reason you might send the food back. If you ordered a rare steak and got it well done, that's one thing. But if, on the other hand, as in the movie *The Jerk,* you ordered escargot, you should not get upset when they bring you snails. In other words, the wine must truly be defective. Just because you don't like it doesn't mean you can send it back. I recall sending only one bottle back in my life. I find that having gone through the trials of being a wine producer, and tasting more and more wines, I can accept a wider spectrum. Also, as technology increases, I encounter few wines with flaws. Then it gets down to a matter of preference.

The one time I sent a wine back, my wife and I were with Professor and Mrs. Harold Olmo. He was my instructor during my Master's work at U.C. Davis. In his experimental program, Dr. Olmo probably tastes more wines in a year than most of us will taste in a lifetime. We were at a small resort area in the middle of nowhere. When the waiter brought the bottle we ordered, the bouquet and taste were badly oxidized. The wine had obviously sat around for a long time. When we told this to the waiter, he said he would have the bartender taste it. Imagine how relieved we were when he came back to announce that the burly bartender agreed. Luckily it was the last bottle so we had to order something else.

43

*"There are more old wine
drinkers than old doctors."*

GERMAN PROVERB

3.
Wine and Your Health

The following quote from the Bishop of Seville makes him my kind of guy:

> "I have enjoyed great health at a great age because every day since I can remember I have consumed a bottle of wine except when I have not felt well. Then I have consumed two bottles."

He sounds like my wine drinking friend, Noah, who lived 950 years. You'll meet him soon.

The healthful aspects of drinking wine are well documented. Hippocrates believed in it as a medicine. He used it with great care and respect, prescribing it as a nourishing dietary beverage, as a cooling agent for fevers, as a purgative and diuretic, and as a dressing for wounds. In this, as in other matters, the teachings of Hippocrates are worthy of his famous oath.

The nutritional value of wine is underlined by the startling fact that—next to milk—wine is the most complex biologic fluid found outside of blood vessels.

The pH of wine (3.0 to 3.5) resembles that of human gastric juice

44

(0.9 to 1.2) more closely than any other beverage. This quality allows it to be easily assimilated.

Wine and winegrowers are the beneficiaries of growing interests in health, diet, exercise and self-improvement.

In considering wine and your health, we must examine both the positive and negative aspects of its consumption. The positive points I make in this chapter are supported by the following generalizations:

1. Moderate drinkers live longer than do either abstainers or heavy drinkers.
2. In the many cases where it is beneficial to health, wine is the active agent; whereas, in the few cases where it is detrimental, it is only the passive agent (i.e. the alcoholic has the "germs" of the illness even before he drinks.)

Let's look first at the health benefits of wine. According to recent research, wine, or wine ingredients, are directly responsible for many healthy effects. The inclusion of wine on the menus at a majority of hospitals in the top 65 U.S. metropolitan population areas seems to be a clear endorsement of wine's beneficial medical effects, or at least of the belief that wine has no negative effects. Wine has been used medicinally throughout history. Only Prohibition interrupted this practice in America. After Prohibition came the technological boom and modern "miracle drugs." The value of wine as medicine lacked the support of scientific research; as a result, it was only recently, when wine came under attack from certain groups, that the wine industry sponsored research to verify what had been known empirically for centuries.

Scientific evidence strongly suggests that moderate consumption of wine is a vital part of reducing overall risk factors for various illnesses and of extending life. Recent research at Stanford University's Center for Research in Disease Prevention, published in the *Journal of the American Medical Association,* showed an "association between moderate alcohol intake and reduced risk of coronary heart disease." This is dramatic evidence supporting the healthful impact of moderate wine consumption against heart disease and heart attacks, the leading killers in America. The reduction of heart disease through the moderate intake of wine is linked to the significant increase of high-density lipoproteins (HDLs). HDLs evidently provide protection against the clogging of coronary arteries by removing cholesterol and other damaging fats that can build up inside artery walls, thereby narrowing the blood vessels. Research indicates that HDLs are increased with the moderate intake of wine and decreased by abstinence from wine.

It has also been shown that polyphenols (color pigment and tannins) reduce blood-cholesterol levels. Anthocyanins and phenolic acids are effective against bacteria and viruses.

Wine has successfully been used to improve appetite and promote digestion among anorexic patients. Obese people, who are trying to stay on diets and lose weight, have found wine effective in their diet, because it acts as an anxiety-relieving tranquilizer.

Wine has been referred to as "the nurse of old age"; it has been especially helpful in the diets of the aged by helping restore nutritional balance, relieve tensions and serve not only as a gentle sedative but as an important euphoric agent.

Simply put, wine is more than just another beverage containing alcohol! There are important distinctions between wine, beer and distilled spirits. Distilled spirits cause higher peak blood alcohol levels, even when diluted to the same concentration as wine and beer; this fact suggests the importance and uniqueness of the non-alcoholic constituents of wine and brew. Let's look for a moment at these non-alcoholic ingredients and the beneficial effects of wine consumption which are attributable to them.

Wine contains over 300 components other than alcohol and provides many minerals and vitamins not found in other. alcoholic beverages. When consumed in moderation with meals, it is an effective aid to digestion and may help reduce the incidence of troublesome sleep disorders.

Natural wines are virtually salt free and, therefore, are prescribed as part of otherwise dull, low sodium diets.

Dry table wine is prescribed in diabetic diets since they serve not only as a source of energy, but can also enhance the flavor of a diet which is, again, exceedingly bland and monotonous. Certain wines also provide sugar or other sources of energy.

Research has revealed the presence of vitamins in wine in small but nutritionally significant amounts. In general, reds contain more vitamins than whites.

Numerous nutritious inorganic elements are naturally present in wine: calcium, copper, iron, iodine, magnesium, phosphorous, zinc, vitamin P, chromium and silicon, all of which have been shown to play important roles in strengthening arterial walls and in preventing heart attack.

Our industry is being pressured to do more medical research to defend itself from critics and to establish itself as the drink of moderation, separate and apart from other beverages containing alcohol. In the long run such investigations will support this difference.

On the other hand, there are patients for whom wine or other drinks containing alcohol should not be used. These include people suffering from peptic ulcer, stomach cancer, pancreatitis, liver problems and inflamations of the mouth, throat, esophagus and stomach. Its use is also questionable in conjunction with acute kidney infection, disorders of the prostate gland, and genito-urinary conditions.

We must also be aware that alcohol may react unpredictably when combined with drugs such as barbiturates, chemical tranquilizers, narcotics and other such agents.

Obviously alcohol should not be used when a person has an uncontrollable drinking problem. This is the most detrimental of all the effects of wine consumption, yet even here it has been shown that moderate wine consumption can decrease risk factors which lead to excessive and abusive drinking. The moderate use of wine, particularly with meals, can develop social and cultural patterns which have been proven to discourage alcohol abuse.

Parents can convey to their children a positive attitude about wine: it is not to be used to become intoxicated. At the same time, I disagree with the thinking that adults should not drink in front of minors during, for example, a dinner involving a youth group. If wine is food, and if we drink it with our meals at home in front of our children, let's be consistent. I consider a bottle of wine as appropriate as I do a loaf of bread (and thou) at a potluck or fund raiser.

Understanding and accepting the fact that alcoholism is a disease should be the single most important objective in educating people about drinking. We are witnessing a growing number of young drinkers in America who understand that it is no longer considered heroic to overindulge. This is true in European nations where alcoholism is not a problem and drunkenness is not considered humorous. The tolerance of drunken behavior is diminishing. Wine as a drink of moderation to be enjoyed with food stands to benefit from this new attitude. Banning wine altogether, or establishing more stringent laws or new taxes, would be like eliminating the automobile because of the number of traffic deaths.

Statistically, it can be demonstrated that alcohol abuse has been decreasing in the United States and that the replacement of the "three-martini lunch" with a glass of wine at a meal is a positive social and cultural trend. Throughout history, intelligent, moderate wine consumption has gone hand in hand with good food and art. We have gone through a period where we lost sight of this. Hopefully we will regain the realization of Dr. Jean Louis Faure, that, "nothing is better to fight alcoholism than the moderate use of wine."

I want to address two subjects in a light, yet serious vein. First is the so called "red-wine headache." Since I make only red wine, this is of interest to me. I wish I could go along with a vintner friend's opinion that such headaches are caused by the olives in the martinis before dinner. After researching the subject, I'm convinced that "red-wine headaches" are real, but only for a small portion of the population. And while I'm not sure we know what causes them, we do know what does not. It is not a hangover. Hangover is correlated to the amount of alcohol consumed and the reaction is delayed. Red-wine headache can be immediate and, for some people, occurs after the consumption of the slightest amount. Negative skin and blood tests also suggest that "red-wine headache" is not due to allergy. In all cases, then, it appears to be dose related. It could be caused by amines or by prostaglandins since, according to medical investigators, it may be prevented in some people by prescribing a prostaglandin inhibitor, such as aspirin or Nuprin® or Advil®.

Actually I'm not sure I know what all that means. Luckily I don't suffer from "red-wine headaches." I do sometimes suffer from a headache caused by enjoying too much wine. But if you are unfortunate enough to suffer from "red-wine headache," the above discussion might shed some light on its causes and prevention.

People, such as my wife, who are hypoglycemic, suffer similar symptoms of headache or "jitters" from the intake of alcohol or from sources of sugar such as desserts.

Even though wine is the drink of moderation, there are times when it tastes so good that we drink too much of it, just as we sometimes overindulge with good food. I must confess I've been know to eat and drink too much. Judging by Americans' waistlines, I'm not alone!

Should you drink too much, you may later experience the unpleasant, though rarely serious, syndrome known as the hangover. Among the possible symptoms are headache, dizziness, nausea, and possibly vomiting, depression and general malaise. A hangover is usually accompanied by low blood sugar values. The symptoms appear many hours after the peak of blood-alcohol concentrations, often the morning after an episode of evening drinking, and are usually most severe when little or no alcohol can be detected in the blood.

The cause of hangover is not known. There is no evidence to support popular notions that it is due simply to the presence of higher alcohols—the so called fusel oils—or other components of the beverage, or to vitamin deficiencies, to dehydration, or to the combination of different beverages. All the theories about mixing drinks causing hangovers are wrong because the syndrome can be produced by any beverage alone or by chemically pure ethyl alcohol.

No satisfactory therapy is known. I'm sure you all have your favorite therapies, whether it be coffee, juice, vitamins or spicy, hot food. Generally, aspirin, bed rest and the ingestion of food and liquids will help.

The one remedy that usually produces relief is more alcohol (a little hair of the dog that bit you). Unfortunately, such treatment is frequently followed by another hangover. I would suggest, instead, that you try to eat and drink moderately.

"People are like wine . . .
Age sours the bad and
improves the good!"
ANONYMOUS

4.
A Brief (and spotty) History of Viticulture and Enology

Serious historians may cringe when they see how I've approached their subject. I'm not concerned about including every important event, nor is chronological accuracy vital to me. I have simply highlighted the events which will give you a feel for the historical development of winegrowing.

Since this chapter is about the history of "viticulture" and "enology," let's start by defining the two terms. "Viticulture," which comes from the Latin word for grapevine, *vitis,* means the culture of the grapevine. "Enology," derived from the Greek word for wine, *Oinos,* is the science of winemaking.

Wine is a natural product, probably developed because grapes and juice didn't keep. Perhaps a caveman smashed some wild grapes but didn't immediately drink the juice. The wild yeast on the grapes fermented the juice to wine and the caveman got a "kick" out of the liquid when he drank it. Wine could be defined, then, as "a beverage resulting from the fermentation by yeast of the juice of the grape with appropriate processing and additions." (Notice that wine is defined as a product of the grape; therefore, by law, if you make wine from any other fruit, you must so state on the label: Apricot Wine, Plum Wine, or whatever other fruit it comes from. The term wine, by itself, like vino, refers to a grape product.)

The earliest references to grapes, in recorded history, are in the Bible, beginning around 3000 B.C. The Bible says that Noah landed on Mount Ararat in the Caucasus Mountains between the Black and Caspian seas in Armenia, and that one of the first things he did was to be a "husbandman to vines" and make wine. (Noah knew it took a little wine to be a good husband.) We might say the modern history of the grape goes back to that time because, obviously, there was a lot of history before Noah, but it got washed out. Will Rogers commented that "the Prohibitionists say that drinking is bad for you but the Bible says that Noah made wine and drank it and he only lived to be 950 years. Show me an abstainer who ever lived that long." I like Will's theology.

So the caveman's wine very likely was the result of an accident. To digress a bit, there are several styles of contemporary wine which were also probably accidents when they were first made. Have you ever heard of Retsina? It's a traditional Greek wine; the word "Retsina" comes from resin. Before bottles were common, people used amphora (a clay jug) as containers for wine. To prevent the amphora from leaking, or possibly to prevent oxidation, early vintners lined the insides of the amphora with resin. The wine picked up the smell and taste of the resin and drinkers got used to it. Even though we now have glass containers, resin is added to the wine to duplicate the wine which retsina drinkers love.

Vermouth, the herb-flavored wine, is another example. It was an accident only insofar as the wine flavor was probably so bad that the only way people could drink it was to add herbs. But even today, with our technology for making non-defective wines, there still is a demand for herb-flavored wine.

Sherry is another accident: it's simply a badly oxidized white wine, or one in which a yeast converts ethyl alcohol to acetaldehyde. Because such wine has become popular, we now take perfectly good products and either bake them or add the yeast in order to produce a traditional Sherry type.

As a final accident, imagine the good monk Dom Perignon. At the monastery, he bottled what he thought was a dry wine, only to have it re-ferment within the corked bottle and produce carbon dioxide. When drunk, it tickled his nose and carried the alcohol more rapidly to his delighted bloodstream. Through a simple error, he had produced champagne, which has become the drink of kings and a favorite on festive occasions.

But winemaking was not entirely a matter of accidents. Egyptian hieroglyphics from 1500 B.C. indicate that the ancients had definite wine-producing strategies. There are descriptions of pruning practices, the use of the press, the production of red and white wines, and even the clever practice of sinking sealed jars in the ground for cool storage.

It seems logical at this point to ask: Why did the grape and wine industries develop? First, because both provided calories and became, important elements in the diet of ancient people. Grapes have the highest sugar content of all fruits, substantially higher than that of sugar beets or sugar cane, which will peak out at 12 to 14 percent sugar, as opposed to the 20 to 24 sugar percentage of a typical grape. In grapes dehydrated to raisins, the sugar content may reach 50 to 75 percent.

Second, early wines were full of vitamins, because they were saturated with yeast cells. Yeast caused the wines to be cloudy, and they were drunk "young," since it was not known how to store them. Otherwise they would spoil.

Another reason for the growth of the industry is that wine has always been fairly antiseptic, in many cases safer than untreated water for you to drink. Louis Pasteur said that "wine is the most hygenic of all beverages." No pathogens have ever been found to live in wine because its low pH and moderate alcohol inhibit growth. And, of course, wine stimulates your appetite, and relaxes you, while the color and taste have aesthetic appeal. Throughout history, too, there has been the mystical connection of blood to red wine, resulting in its use in many religious services. Water was frequently added to vino, either to purify the water or to water down bad wine. This practice also prevented drunkenness.

Perhaps the Romans were the first to classify grape varieties. They invented the pruning knife, discovered the use of fertilization and the pasteurization of wines in a smokehouse for stability. They used alkali to reduce acidity, gypsum to raise acidity, saltwater to improve color, the use of spices and herbs to enhance flavor, and were the first to record the use of bottles and wine glasses. The Romans carried viticulture and enology into France, Germany, and England. But just as it can today, winemaking tended to bring about competition, pettiness, and bickering. Roman scribes, possibly the first wine writers, criticized the wines of France. In the first century, Emperor Probrius even prohibited the growing of grapes in France. Perhaps Probrius simply wanted wheat or some other crop to be grown there, but maybe it was that the French wines were better than those of Rome.

Many references to grapes and wine appear in the Bible. Christ,

Himself, performed His first miracle at Cana, converting water to wine in order to prevent embarrassment of a host who had run out at a wedding feast. The Bureau of Alcohol, Tobacco and Firearms probably would have declared Christ's miracle at Cana an illegal winemaking practice. (I like the somewhat irreverent joke about Joseph drinking too much vino at the wedding feast because it was so good. The next morning because he had a headache and a dry mouth, he asked Mary for a glass of water but cautioned, "For goodness sakes, don't let Jesus touch it.") Christ also suggested in a parable that new wine not be put into old goatskins (bota bags) which may indicate that it was already common knowledge that fermentation gave off carbon dioxide gas. The old bags, which were inflexible, would explode if used. Finally, He used wine at the Last Supper with His followers. When He passed the cup and said, "Do this in My memory," wine became an integral part of Christian church liturgy.

The monks of the Middle Ages made wine not only for sacramental purposes but also for their own table use, and thus played an important part in preserving the vineyards of France, Spain, Germany, Austria, and Yugoslavia. In their archives, they also recorded much of the known winemaking technology of that day. Thirteenth-century Crusaders are credited with having brought many grape varieties from the Middle East. Africa was one of the last areas to promulgate the grape, due to the the Islamic prohibition of alcohol. It is interesting, however, that even though the Koran forbids alcohol, it promises the faithful Muslim that when he goes to his eternal reward, "he will drink wine from gold and silver cups and have rivers of milk and honey."

Moving through history quickly, we find that by 1850 grapes were grown and wine was made in all parts of the world, from the 51st degree N. latitude in Germany, to the 45th degree S. latitude in New Zealand. Unfortunately, because of the lack of winemaking knowledge then, at least 25 percent of all wine was spoiled shortly after the end of fermentation.

In 1810, Gay-Lussac accurately described the primary fermentation of sugar to ethyl alcohol and carbon dioxide gas. (Still, he couldn't figure out how Christ did it with water.) Louis Pasteur, between 1861 and 1870, made several important discoveries. He also drank his share of wine. His first major insight was that the primary fermentation of sugar to alcohol was an anaerobic fermentation, which means that it did not require oxygen to function. He later found that acetic acid bacteria converted alcohol to acetic acid (vinegar). The latter is an aerobic reaction, which means that it does require oxygen, so this discovery was a great step forward. The elimination of oxygen, achieved primarily by keeping containers full, would go a long way toward eliminating the unintentional conversion of wine to vinegar.

In the mid-1800s, the grape industry was plagued with downy mildew, powdery mildew, and black rot. In 1870, an even greater disaster occurred when native eastern-American grapevines taken to Europe transported microscopic Phylloxera (root louse). Between 1870 and 1910, most French, German, Austrian, and California vineyards were destroyed; later, it was found possible to overcome Phylloxera by planting native American vines and then grafting to them the European variety above the ground. However, there was a beneficial effect of the Phylloxera problem; most vineyards were deliberately replanted, resulting in fewer but better varieties.

California's grape and wine history, began in 1769. During that year in San Diego at the first of the missions, Father Junipero Serra planted the Mission variety of grapevine called Criolla (meaning "native" in many parts of the world). As the Franciscans established other missions up the California coast, they planted vineyards. Sacramental wine was required for religious ceremonies; besides, those pioneers had been accustomed to wine with their meals in Europe. Brandy was distilled from wine at the missions and used for trading purposes. The largest mission vineyard was established in Southern California at San Gabriel. In 1833, Mexico took over California and secularized the missions. The vineyards deteriorated after that but the Franciscans can claim credit for having shown the possibilities for grape growing and brandy production in California.

In the 1830s, Jean Louis Vignes imported Vinifera (European) vines and planted them in the first important vineyard in the Los Angeles area. William Wolfskill, another pioneer, established an early vineyard in Winters, not too far from Sacramento. In the 1850s, Agoston Haraszthy, one of the most colorful characters in the history of the California grape industry, arrived on the scene. After first settling in San Diego, he moved north to San Mateo, planting vineyards in both places. In 1857, Haraszthy made his way to the Sonoma Valley where he established the Buena Vista Winery. A pamphlet he published in 1858 led to the establishment of a committee to study grape production in California. In 1860 Haraszthy was able to convince Governor William Downey to send him to Europe to gather and bring back cuttings of various European varieties. When he returned in 1862 with some 200,000, Downey had been voted out of office and the legislature refused to pay Haraszthy for his trip. (For this, Downey Mildew was named after the governor.) Haraszthy, meanwhile, sold his cuttings around California to cover his costs. He thus became instrumental in spreading Vinifera varieties throughout the state. For good reason, he has been acclaimed as the "father" of California viticulture. Later Haraszthy became the Director of the San Francisco Mint but was indicted when he could not account for $100,000 in missing gold. However, he was not convicted. Toward the end of his life, Haraszthy went off to South America where, it is said, he was eaten by crocodiles. Considering the wine he had imbibed, Haraszthy probably provided the crocodiles with a well-marinated meal!

Vineyards increased all over California between 1860 and 1900. General Mariano Vallejo, for instance, planted some around Sonoma. John Sutter had vineyards, a winery and distillery in Sacramento. Senator Leland Stanford started a vineyard and, at the time, claimed the world's largest winery in Vina, near Chico in Northern California. The Wentes settled and developed viticulture in Livermore. George Yount, after whom Yountville, in the Napa Valley, was named, was Napa's first grape grower in 1838, and also made the first documented Napa Valley wine in 1853. Charles Krug, in 1861, was the second winegrower in the Napa Valley. Early grape-growing and winemaking names in the now industry-famous Napa Valley were George Crane, Gustav Niebaum, Jacob and Frederick Beringer, Jacob Schram, and Gottlieb Groezinger. During the 1880s, some beautiful wineries were built in the Napa Valley, many of which still stand. Between 1882 and 1883, for example, W. H. Bourne built the Greystone Cellars (now the cellars of the Christian Brothers) which,

1883 RHINE HOUSE, BERINGER HOME

at that time, was the largest stone building under a single roof in the world. Other beautiful architectural statements of the era were those of Beringer, Chateau Chevalier, Inglenook, Krug, Far Niente and Eshcol (now Trefethen).

A directory of Napa Valley growers in 1890 shows that nearly every vineyard grew Zinfandel, that almost as many boasted Riesling, and that well over half had Chasselas (Palomino). H. H. Crabb had more than 200 varieties growing in the mid-1880s at his ToKallon Vineyard in Oakville. Niebaum at Inglenook was storing, in a private library, Cabernet Sauvignons from the 1880s and 1890s; all this activity seems to indicate that Napa Valley growers were trying to determine what varieties it could best produce. But by the 1880s, with 12,000 acres of grapes planted in the valley, an oversupply of wine resulted and bulk wine was selling at 10 to 15 cents per gallon. During the same period, to amend the problem, the California legislature provided funds for viticulture and enology research, and a board of state viticultural commissioners was established. At the same time, Professor Eugene Hilgard at the University of California was experimenting with the adaptation of various grape varieties to diverse climatic regions; he was trying to determine the proper maturity level for the harvest of California grapes. Then, during the late 1870s and 1880s, Phylloxera (root louse) began to attack and kill vineyards in both Europe and California.

During that same period, several grape-growing colonies were established in California, and became important to the state's viticultural history. The Anaheim colony, near Los Angeles, primarily a German settlement, established some 1800 acres of vineyard. It developed one of the best and most progressive irrigation systems of its time. The vineyards were destroyed by what was called "Anaheim" disease (later identified as Pierce Disease), for which we are just learning the cause and preventive measures. An even larger settlement of 4,000 acres was begun at Guasti in Southern California, while, in approximately 1893, the Italian Swiss Colony was established at Asti, north of San Francisco, and grew to 2,000 acres of vineyard.

The wine industry did well in the first and second decades of the 1900s, but with the ratification of the Eighteenth Amendment on January 29, 1919, and the Prohibition era that followed, winemakers had to leave the industry to find other jobs. Cooperage (wooden containers such as barrels and tanks) went bad from being dried out, and distribution systems disappeared. A few wineries were able to stay open to provide wines for sacramental and medicinal purposes. Strangely enough, however, the planting of grapes actually increased during Prohibition, since it was permissible for any family to make 200 gallons of vino for private consumption. Grapes were being shipped in boxes all over the United States from California for home production purposes. Unfortunately, the most popular grapes were not those that made the best wine but those which best kept and shipped. Zinfandel was quite popular but probably the most desirable was Alicante. It is a grape rarely used anymore because of its mediocre quality but its popularity in those days derived from the fact that it was one of the few varieties that contained red juice; therefore, home winemakers could squeeze the grapes and make one batch of red wine out of the juice, then add back water, sugar, and acid to the red skins and extract the color from the skins to make a second batch. (350 gallons vs 175 gallons per ton of grapes.) It is said that during Prohibition a cutting of the Alicante grapevine, which could be planted to grow a new vine, sold for one dollar.

Naturally, after Repeal of Prohibition by the Twenty-First Amendment in 1933, the wine industry had a lot of reorganizing to do. Because much of the cooperage had gone bad, and because most of the technical people had left the industry, many poor wines were produced at the beginning of that period. One well-known vintner is quoted as saying that the wines of that period were "something like grape juice in December and something like vinegar in June." Except for some artificially elevated demands caused by World War II, the fine wine market sagged through the 1940s and 1950s. The California Wine Institute, with its technical and legislative committees, and the Wine Advisory Board worked hard during this period of adjustment to get the industry back on track. Researchers at the University of California at Davis helped refine the art of wine production and trained many young vintners. In the 1960s, higher alcohol dessert and appetizer wines were still more popular than table wines. In the 1970s, however, the pendulum swung away from the former until, in the mid to late 70s, more table wines were sold than dessert wines.

While generic wines (common red, white and roses not named after a specific grape variety) continued to provide more volume than varietals (wines produced from the grape variety after which they are named), the latter have since become much more popular with wine fanciers. As for the future of fine wine, I think that you can expect this trend to continue for a long time to come.

*"The blood of the vineyard
shall mingle with mine."*

OLIVER WENDELL HOLMES

5.

The Anatomy of a Grapevine

Since I first began to study the grapevine some twenty-five years ago, I have found it a fascinating and unique plant. I'm going to discuss some of its specific anatomical features, with the hope that through understanding the grapevine—how it functions, how it produces quality fruit—you can better appreciate your wine.

I respect the grapevine because it's hardy and tough, attributes I like to believe that I have too. The grapevine can survive under more varied growing conditions than any other plant in the world. Once started, it can put down a root system 30 or more feet deep in order to find the water and nutrients it needs to survive. So, usually, it's not a matter of whether or not a grapevine will grow in a specific area, but simply a question of its ability to produce quality fruit and quality wine within that area. For instance, Cabernet Sauvignon will grow quite well and produce a sizable crop in the warm Central Valley of California. Yet to produce the best quality red table wine, it prefers a cooler climate such as the Napa Valley. There it may give only one-half the crop it would yield in the warm Central Valley, but will reward the grower with superior quality. As a rule, then, when quantity and sugar-content are desirable, such as in table grapes, the warmer growing areas are preferable; somewhat cooler regions generally produce higher quality fruit. A cooler region yet may have a tendency to produce fruit and wines with exotic aromas and flavors, exotic to the point of dulling the palate and thus becoming less desirable. As for the grapevine itself, it is versatile and extremely forgiving.

I remember once accepting the challenge to hike in one day from the rim of the Grand Canyon down to the Colorado River and back. The round trip is some twelve miles and the vertical drop is 5,000 feet. I did it with only a chocolate bar and an orange in my pocket, not knowing that there were only two water stops on the way. I can tell you that when I crawled over the rim at 6:00 that evening, a six-pack of beer sounded much better to me than a fine bottle of Cabernet Sauvignon! But besides the incredible beauty of the Grand Canyon, I was fascinated by two other things. One was the sign which explained that in the 5,000 foot drop, you traveled through five different climatic zones, which otherwise you could experience only by trekking from the Grand Canyon to the Equator. The other thing that fascinated me was my discovery of wild grapevines growing along the pathway about half way down the Canyon. I brought a sample back to U.C., Davis and learned from Professor Olmo that it was Vitis Arizonica, a native grapevine of that area. I decided that if a grapevine could grow there, it could grow almost anywhere!

I think it's important in this section to include a brief explanation about the botanical classification of the grapevine.

Order	*Rhamnales*
Class	*Dicotyledoneae*
Division	*Spermatophyta—Angiospermae*
Family	*Vitaceae*
Genus	*Vitis*
Species	*Vinifera*

This part may seem a bit academic, but I want to show you where the grapevine fits in the plant world. The class Dicotyledoneae simply indicates that it's more complex than a simple grass. As a Spermatophyta, that it's a seed plant, and the term Angiospermae just means that it's a protected seed, protected by the flesh of the grape berry, rather than existing exposed. Now, when we get to family, the fancy words become more important. Vitaceae indicates that it's a vine; it's a vine because it climbs, and it climbs because it has tendrils (which we will discuss in a moment), which give all vines the ability to cling.

If you come to the Napa Valley, you'll find many of the old stone wineries covered with other types of vines in the Vitaceae family, notably Parthenosis (Virginia Creeper) and Ivy. While the tendrils of the grapevine need to wrap around something, such as a trellis wire, the Virginia Creeper has suction cups which emit a sticky substance that gives it the ability to attach to a flat wall. It is green in the summer and turns to spectacular reds and yellows in the fall. It seems fitting that the walls of a winery should be decorated by another member of the vine family. That brings us to the genus Vitis, which makes it specifically a grapevine, only one of eleven of the genera Vitaceae. Finally we arrive at the species Vitis Vinifera. I will be referring specifically to vinifera, but some people prefer to call it the "European" grape. Within the species Vinifera are such varieties as Chardonnay, Chenin Blanc, White Riesling, Gewürztraminer, and Sauvignon Blanc, to name just a few of the white varieties. Pinot Noir, Zinfandel, Gamay, Mérlot, and Cabernet Sauvignon are among some of the reds. All were brought to America from somewhere in Europe.

Other species of Vitis include Vitis Labrusca, the grape of the eastern U.S., of which the Concord is possibly the best known variety; Vitis Rotundifolia, a species of the Southeast United States; Vitis Rupestris, from which several of the Phylloxera-resistant root stocks were hybridized; the previously mentioned Vitis Arizonica, and Vitis Californica, obviously native to that state. The latter is the grapevine you frequently see if you drive around Northern California. It grows wild and does particularly well near creek and river beds. The reason you rarely see fruit on this variety is that in contrast to the Vinifera, the Californica does not have both the male and female parts on the same flower and, therefore, requires cross pollination.

Another way to distinguish grape varieties is by the recognizable flavors of their fruit. The first division includes the following:

1. **Distinctive non-vinifera**
   This is typified by the Concord or the Scuppernong; both are grapes with strong varietal aromas and flavors.
2. **Distinctive Vinifera**
   a. *Muscat:* This variety is in a class by itself as a Vinifera because of its distinctive aroma. You owe it to yourself to smell and taste one of the distinctive Muscats produced. Usually they are on the sweeter side and, thus, are to be enjoyed as dessert or appetizer wines. They may variously be called Muscat Canelli, Muscato di Canelli, some derivative of the previous two, or by proprietary names such as Château La Salle or Muscato D' Oro.
   b. *Other Vinifera varietals:* These have their own distinct identifiable characteristics, such as Chardonnay, Sauvignon Blanc, White Riesling, Zinfandel, and Cabernet Sauvignon.
3. **Non-distinctive Vinifera**
   In this category are varieties producing wines that would be difficult, if not impossible, to identify in a blind tasting; some examples are Thompson Seedless, Chasselas, or Alicante Boushet.

Now let's look at some illustrations while we discuss the specific anatomy of a grapevine. This section will appeal to readers interested in plants and, those trying to grow, train, and prune a grapevine; it should also be helpful, I hope, to the artists among my readers who wish to draw or paint the grapevine. One of my pet peeves as a viticulturist is to see an artist's depiction of the grapevine which makes it appear to be an ivy plant, a Virginia Creeper, or some other type of vine. When we inspect the shoot and leaves together, we'll see some of the specifics which I not only find fascinating but which make the grapevine unique and identifiable.

Take a look at Illustration #1, showing the grapevine as it might appear in the winter when it is dormant. Note first something very important to the grapevine, but not observable: the root system. These roots, which, as I mentioned earlier, may go as deep as 30 feet, serve two important functions. First, they anchor the grapevine; second; they absorb from the soil the moisture and nutrients vital to the life of a vine.

Occasionally I have seen eroded hillsides with vines with as much as 10 feet of exposed roots. These would normally not be seen, yet

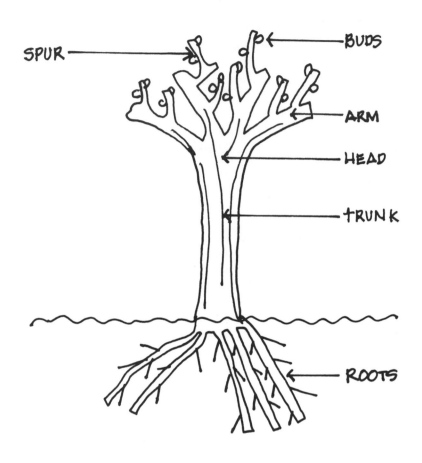

ILLUSTRATION I

because there were far more roots deeper in the soil, the vine continued to live and function normally. It could not do so forever since most of the feeder roots are in the top few feet of soil. Such a case does, however, illustrate the hardiness of the grapevine.

In the above-ground portion of the vine you first see the trunk, or the undivided part of the vine from the ground to the head. Next comes the head or the branching part of the grapevine. Arms are the short branches extending from the head; we reserve the term branches for that part of the growth longer than the arms, such as are found on a cordon, which we will discuss in Chapter 7. The shoot is the green extension of growth seen in the spring; the cane is the previous year's green shoot which has since become one year old mature wood and which contains within its buds next year's crop. A spur is a mature cane cut back to a few buds. Water sprouts (not shown) are shoots coming out of wood more than one year old but usually not from dormant buds. Such sprouts are commonly referred to by growers as "suckers." Strictly speaking, however, a sucker is growth from underground.

In the same Illustration, you can see in the dormant vine, that buds are located on alternating sides of either the short spurs or the canes. Let us suppose that we focused in on any one bud on the dormant vine. You will see in Illustration #2 how this growthpoint swells and begins to grow during the spring. Notice that each one contains within itself the primordia (beginnings) of shoot, leaves, tendrils, clusters, and buds which will, in turn, form the next year's growth and crop. The shoot of a vine grows from the bud, much in the same fashion as a telescope extends. The first part out will always be the furthermost extension. However, the first bud laid will remain at the base of the shoot, with others, along with leaves, clusters and tendrils being added as the shoot elongates. Its tip is the terminal bud which expresses the elongation of the growth. The nodes are simply positions along the shoot where the leaf, the dormant bud, and the active bud are located. The space between the nodes is termed the internode. The angle formed between the leaf stem and the shoot is called the axil. Within the axil are two buds: the active, or axillary bud, and the dormant bud. This dormant bud is the most important

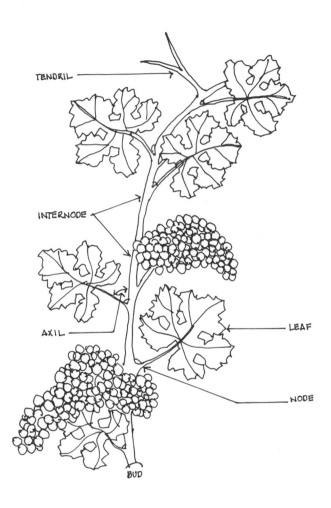

ILLUSTRATION 2

because it enlarges, matures, and contains within itself next year's growth and crop. The active or axillary bud will generally remain dormant, unless the dormant bud is injured or unless the vine has excessive vigor, in which case the active bud forms lateral growth. Next, notice that coming down the shoot, the leaves alternate sides. This is one of the specifics of the grapevine. Notice also that there is a leaf at every node. Opposite most leaves are the tendrils which make the grape a vine and which give it the ability to climb.

The tendril is one of the characteristics which makes the Vinifera grapevine identifiable among other species. At every third position, the Vinifera has a discontinuous tendril. This is significant because a cluster of grapes is nothing more than a well-developed tendril; that is, it's one that flowers and fruits. There are usually two to three positions at the base of each shoot which have such clusters. On close examination, you'll find the stem of such a cluster to be simply a tendril. In the case of the discontinuous example, starting with the first cluster at the base of the shoot, you'll find a well-developed tendril (or cluster) up on one of the alternating sides of the shoot. Up a step higher, you will find a similar cluster on the alternating side of the shoot. At the next position up, you will find no tendril at all opposite the leaf. It is this feature of the discontinuous tendril that gives it its name; it is also one of the identifying characteristics of the Vinifera that makes it different from other species of grapevines. Proceeding up the shoot, you will find a first tendril, a second, and a blank. No matter how long the shoot grows, whether it be 3 or 15 feet, the pattern of the discontinuous tendril at every third node will recur.

The other pattern that close examination reveals is that the length of the internodes at the base of the shoot are short, indicative of the cooler temperatures during the spring. In the center of the shoot, on the other hand, the internodes will be longer because of the optimum and desirable growing conditions of the summer. Toward the fall, as the vine runs out of moisture and warmth, the internodes will shorten at the tip of the shoot.

Illustration #3 is a magnification of the node. It shows that the shoot or cane swells at the node position. Coming out of one side of the node is a cluster or a tendril. Opposite is a leaf. The leaf stem is

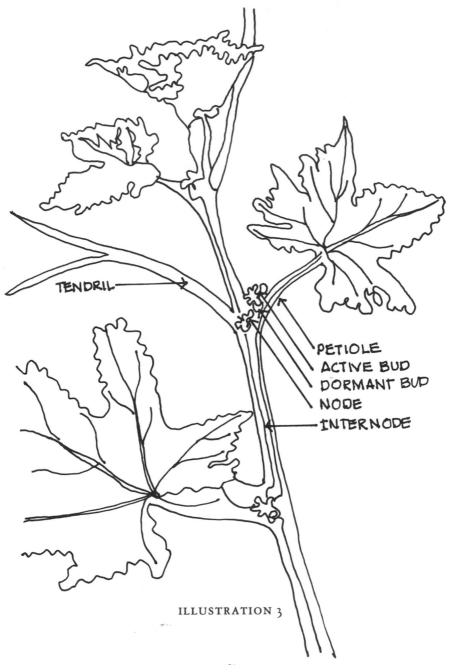

TENDRIL

PETIOLE
ACTIVE BUD
DORMANT BUD
NODE
INTERNODE

ILLUSTRATION 3

called the petiole. The petiole not only supports the leaf blade, but translocates moisture and nutrients from the root system to the leaf. It also translocates sugar, manufactured in the leaf, back into the vines, particularly to the fruit and the root system, to store for the following year. Because the petiole translocates many of the nutrients during the springtime, it is common practice when the grape flower is in bloom to take a sample of petioles for analysis in the laboratory. From this it can be determined whether or not the vine is getting from the soil enough of the various nutrients, such as nitrogen, potassium, and phosphorus.

Illustration #4 is a close-up of the grape leaf. Again you have the stem or petiole. The petiolar sinus is the angle between the petiole and the leaf blade. This angle is sometimes important in the identification of specific grape varieties. The magic number for the leaf is five because there are five veins emanating from the area where the leaf blade is attached to the petiole. Some of the other vines, such as the Virginia Creeper and Ivy, have a main vein, with the other veins branching away from it; in the grapevine, the five

4. CABERNET SAUVIGNON

main veins emanate from the same point. The entire flat part of the leaf is referred to as the blade; the lobes are the meaty portion of the blade which fill in around each vein. The concave angles where the lobes meet are referred to as the sinuses.

While these terms may seem esoteric, they are vital in the identification of various grape varieties. If you are a grape buyer, for instance, it is important that you be able to tell the difference in the field between Cabernet Sauvignon, Zinfandel, and Pinot Noir, since the price per-ton might vary quite significantly among them, and certainly the quality and character of the wine you make will be totally different. Here, for instance, are some of the identifying characteristics of the Cabernet: it is a black grape with medium-sized clusters; the leaf has deep sinuses and there is a naked vein at the petiolar sinus. The Chardonnay leaf, on the other hand, is almost round. On close inspection you can see sinuses, but they are so slight that the leaf appears more circular. The Chardonnay is one of the few other varieties, besides Cabernet, which has the naked vein at the petiolar sinus. Is it only coincidence that the most sought after white and the most desired red varieties have this common characteristic of identification?

There are five types of buds on a grapevine. Terminal buds cause shoots to elongate. The following year's crop is within the enlarged and matured dormant buds. An active bud grows if a terminal bud is injured or if the vine has excessive vigor. Collar buds are the small cottony buds at the base of a shoot. Generally they have no function in the year that they appear, but Mother Nature has a plan. Frequently, because they are so close to the base of the shoot, they are not pruned off and, in the years that follow, they become covered by bark. Collar buds are then sometimes referred to as senescent buds; it is from the latter that water sprouts or "suckers" develop. When they appear in useful places, they are not suckered off (removed) but are trained to be replacement canes.

Let's take a look at the grape flower in Illustration #5 for a minute. This blossom does not pop open as do many ornamental flowers; rather, it has a cap or callyptra which comes off the top like a stocking cap or like an upsidedown cup on a saucer, exposing the grape flower (Illustration #5a & 5b). Within it are both the female and male parts.

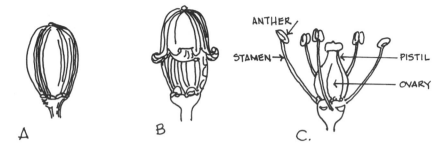

ILLUSTRATION 5

Therefore, cross-pollination is not necessary as is the case in many fruit trees. The female part of the blossom is called the pistil, within which is the ovary. The male part of the flower is the anther, supported to the height of the pistil by the stamen (5c). The grape bloom is not much bigger than a pinhead, so even the slightest wind can cause the pollen from the anther to float over and catch on the sticky substance at the top of the pistil. Pollen then works its way down and pollinates the ovary. When this happens, the flower is "set." Ovaries become the seeds of the berry and the pistil expands to become the grape berry itself. "Poor set" refers to a situation in which few ovaries on a cluster are successfully pollinated, resulting in straggly clusters with few berries. This could be caused by heat, wind, or by rainy conditions at bloomtime.

Finally, let's focus on a cross section of a shoot, cane, or trunk in Illustration #6. As with any growing plant, there are three important layers. The first, cambium, is responsible for the increase in girth. It divides twice a year, once to the inside, producing the xylem, and again to the outside, producing the phloem. The trick in successful budding or grafting is to match the cambium cells of the resistant rootstock and scion variety in order for it to "take." The xylem is the water-conducting tissue which brings moisture and nutrients from the roots up into the plant, without which the plant can neither grow nor produce sugar. The phloem is the downward-conducting tissue

71

which brings to the rest of the plant the sugar and acid manufactured in the leaf. At the end of each growing season, the plant must accumulate enough sugar in its roots to have the energy to start its own growth the following spring, until it has produced enough leaves to manufacture sugar. Each year new phloem is produced and the old phloem is sloughed off to the outside, becoming bark. There is a practice in the production of table grapes called "girdling," which refers to using a special knife to cut a ring around the trunk of the vine in order to prevent the phloem from conducting sugar downward into the roots. This causes the post-girdling sugar production to be accumulated in the fruit, causing a higher and quicker maturity in the table grapes.

So there you have a crash course in grapevine physiology. I hope it will be of some use, especially to the artists, so that depictions of grapevines will start looking more like actual grapevines. If you draw five veins from one point, have five lobes flanking the veins, and five sinuses, you've got a grape leaf. The rest is up to you!

ILLUSTRATION 6

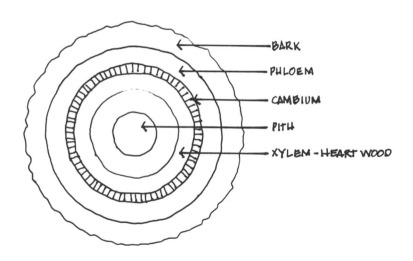

BARK
PHLOEM
CAMBIUM
PITH
XYLEM - HEART WOOD

Rain makes the vines grow,
the vines make the wine flow,
Oh Lord! Let it rain!

ANONYMOUS

6.

The Grapevine at Work

Now that you have a better idea of a grapevine's structure, let's discuss how it functions. Sugar and acid, both very important in the quality determination of grapes and wine, are manufactured by the grapevine. We will look at them separately and examine the factors which both contribute to and inhibit the production of sugar and acid.

Sugar is produced in plants through the photosynthetic process. The plant takes water from the soil, carbon dioxide from the air, uses light as its source of energy, and within the chloroplast of the plant, converts water and carbon dioxide to sugar and oxygen. The berry receives the sugar, and the oxygen is given back to the atmosphere. When we breathe oxygen we give off carbon dioxide; if it weren't for the plants, we would eventually asphyxiate ourselves.

PHOTOSYNTHESIS

$$\text{Water + Carbon Dioxide} \xrightarrow[\text{Chloroplast}]{\text{Light}} \text{Sugar + Oxygen}$$

$$(6H_2O) + (6CO_2) \longrightarrow (C_6H_{12}O_6) + (6O_2)$$

If we understand the formula above, we understand the need for many vineyard cultural practices discussed in the next chapter. For instance, since water is essential for the life and sugar production of the plant, we must remove weeds which compete with the plant for the available moisture in the soil. Also, we need green leaves to capture the sunlight. The red and blue rays of the sun raise the chlorophyll electron to a higher state of energy and this energy drives the photosynthetic reaction. Therefore, we work to prevent the leaves from being damaged by insects or nutrient deficiencies, or from falling off from lack of water, or from changing to any color other than green due to virus, insects, or other causes; otherwise, we won't have an efficient sugar-producing factory.

With the advent of virus-free plants in the last few years, we see vines that retain their greenness until the first frost comes in the fall. Granted, they are not nearly as spectacular as the beautiful red, orange, and yellow colors that we saw in the old vines, but remember—whenever you see those beautiful autumn colors, you can be sure that the grapevines are virused and will have trouble maturing their crop.

As with all chemical reactions, the photosynthetic process is influenced by heat. Cooler temperatures will slow it down, while warmer temperatures, to a point, will speed it up. Research shows that the vine does not enjoy extreme temperatures. That is why it becomes dormant in the winter and only begins to grow when the average temperature is above 50° Fahrenheit (F). Somewhere near 95° F, the vine becomes too warm and does not care to work any longer. Optimal temperatures for the functioning of the grapevine are probably between 70° and 90° F.

You can easily see the importance in sugar production for the green leaves to capture the sunlight which drives the photosynthetic reaction. Trellis systems are commonly used to help in this process, and are discussed further in the next chapter. Simply stated, the purpose of the trellis system is to spread the leaves out to eliminate shading so that as many leaves as possible will capture sunlight, enabling the grapevine to work at maximum efficiency. This assumes, of course, that we have decent light. It also means that sugar is not produced in the vine at night.

We have looked at the optimum-working temperatures and learned that water and carbon dioxide are essential. Sometimes people ask me how harmful air pollution is to the plants. The answer is—very. Several years ago, some extremely sick grapevines in Riverside County of Southern California were enclosed in a glass house so that the air could be filtered to eliminate pollutants. Within a brief time the quantity and quality of the fruit increased dramatically. It makes you wonder: if the Southern California air can so sicken a grapevine, what does it do to us?

The other important product of the grapevine is acid. When we speak of acid, we aren't talking about something which is going to attack the enamel of your teeth. We're referring to several that are produced within the grapevine. The first is citric acid, which you commonly experience in the sourness of a lemon; the second is malic, which you encounter in the crispness of an apple; the third is tartaric in a grape, which causes it to taste sour when it is green, and which, when low, as in an overripe grape, results in a flat taste.

Acidity is produced within the mitochondria of the leaves in a chemical reaction referred to as Kreb's Cycle, depicted below:

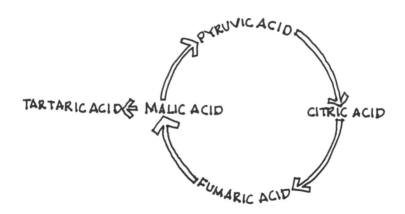

When the vine is not under stress, the citric, tartaric, and malic acids will accumulate in the berries through production in the leaves. As the berries grow in size, if the vine has too much water, the acid supply may diminish simply through dilution, because the berries grow faster than acid accumulates. If the berries were to shrivel through dehydration, acidity would increase.

Heat is the major form of stress affecting acid production. When the weather gets too warm, the plant undergoes a process called respiration, which is roughly equivalent to our panting or sweating under stress. During respiration, citric and malic acid are burnt off and diminish in quantity. In order to reduce respiration (as well as sunburn), it is common to sprinkle plants when the temperature rises above 95° F.

The following diagram illustrates how during the ripening season in the summer, the grape berry grows from a small, hard, green BB-size, with no sugar but sourly acidic, to a full-size, sweet version possessing desirable sugar/acid balance.

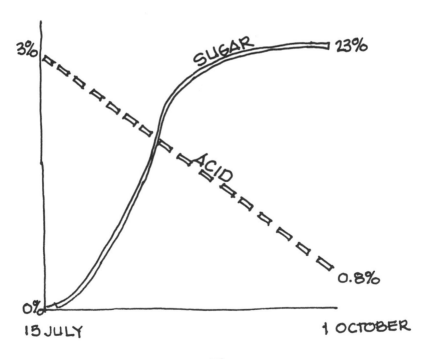

Since respiration goes on all summer, the acid drop is constant; at the same time, the berry is increasing in size, causing the acid to comprise a lesser percentage of the total content. On the other hand, the sugar production starts slowly, accumulates more rapidly during August, then begins to slow down again as the vine runs out of moisture and begins to accumulate sugar in parts of the vine other than the fruit. These other parts—such as roots, trunk, and canes—are called "sinks," since they catch sugar and other carbohydrates in order to give the vine enough energy to begin growth the following spring before there are any leaves.

Sugar production is the most important single factor in the determination of maturity of fruit. If you are eating fruit, you want it sweet. Sugar makes it tasty and gives you energy. As explained in the next chapter, if you're making wine from the grapes, sugar is directly converted to ethyl alcohol by a specific chemical process. Thus, if the vintner knows how much alcohol makes his particular variety of wine taste best, he can determine the sugar-level at which to harvest the grapes.

There are two ways of measuring acid and, therefore, two ways of speaking about it. The first is total acidity, which is the measure of total titratable hydrogen ions; the second is pH, which is the measure of free hydrogen ions on a logarithmic scale. Although in total acidity a higher number indicates more acid, you must understand that in pH, water is neutral at 7, anything below that number is acidic. The amount of hydrogen ions increase, then, as you go down the scale. 3.2 pH, for instance, will be more acidic than 3.5 pH. pH has a lot to do with the longevity of a wine. In California, for example, wines with a pH of 3.2 to 3.5 are generally considered desirable. Below 3.0 the wines might have a very hard and "steely" character. Wines above 3.5 pH are sometimes called "flabby."

You will find, though, that balance of sugar and acid is the key to the proper maturity of grapes and the quality of wines. It is inaccurate to say that 0.75 total acidity makes a better wine than 0.65 total acidity, without considering the other factors that bring about balance. By the same token, however, the alcohol content of a wine means little when not considered in light of acid, tannin, and other flavor components. Yes, a low alcohol wine may taste thin or watery while a high alcohol wine may be hot or overpowering, but I have begun to think that putting the alcohol content on the label of a bottle of wine can be counterproductive because in itself it means nothing. Many a consumer forms a preconceived notion of quality based on the alcohol content. Eleven to 14 percent alcohol is considered the table wine category because at this alcohol level wine complements food. You commonly find on the labels of some of the finest European wines the simple statement "Table Wine," indicating that it is in the 11 to 14 percent alcohol range. I like that practice (French winegrowers aren't all bad) and, although it's not common presently in California, I think it will be in the future. We need to show that flavor and balance are more important than a single factor—namely alcohol content.

A VINE'S ANNUAL CYCLE

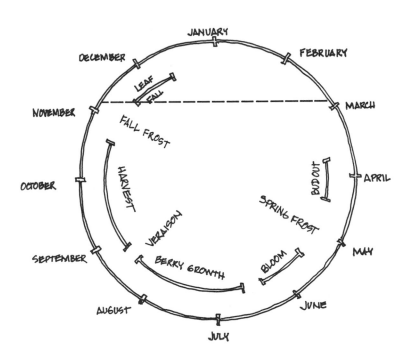

Finally, take a look at the annual cycle of a vine illustrated here. Please understand that the cycle represents the northern hemisphere, which includes the best known vineyards of Europe and the United States. Grape-growing regions in the Southern Hemisphere, such as South America, Australia, and New Zealand, have their growing season during our winter months.

The upper half of the circle, November to March, indicates the dormancy portion of the year and the beginning of a new annual cycle. Grapevines shed leaves with the coming of the first frost, wind, and rains in November or December. To the untrained eye, a vine may look dead after leaves fall but, come spring, when the root temperature rises above 50° F, the vines begin to grow or "bud out." During the months of April and May, when we have young succulent growth at the same time that we have nights with temperatures falling below 32° F, there is a frost danger. If a vine experiences 31° F for a half hour, it will be frosted and its entire crop lost. Therefore, frost protection is necessary in many of the grape-growing regions of the world. In late May to early June, grape flowers bloom and self-pollinate, "setting" the crop for the year. From mid-June to mid-August, berries increase in size but are still green and hard. Sometime in August a dramatic change called "Veraison" occurs. Berries start to soften and change color from hard green to red in red grapes, and from hard green to a soft green or yellowish in white grapes. After Veraison there is a rapid increase in sugar content until the berries are determined mature and ready for harvest. Maturity is a subjective term and can be different for each variety, including table grapes and raisin grapes. Even different wine varieties may have independent maturity standards, which we will discuss in another chapter.

You should also understand that different grapes ripen at different times of the season. Varieties such as Gewürztraminer, Sauvignon (Fumé) Blanc, Chardonnay, and Pinot Noir are considered early varieties and, in California, tend to ripen from late August to mid-September. Cabernet Sauvignon is one of the latest to ripen, maturing from early October to early November. Other varieties tend to ripen between the two extremes. Many times in this state we must race to pick late varieties, such as Cabernet, before November rains come. A year such as 1972 was considered inferior for Cabernet Sauvignon because the heavy rain experienced before the grapes were gathered caused dilution of the sugar and acids and created substantial rot problems. After the vintage the first frost comes, wind and rain knock the leaves off, vines go dormant and another annual cycle begins.

Now you know what the vine looks like and have some basic comprehension of how it functions. In the next chapter you can read about some of the important factors you'd consider if you wanted to be, or are, a grape grower.

*Make the vine poor and
it will make you rich.*

—ANONYMOUS

7.
It All Starts in the Vineyards
(So you want to grow grapes?)

Quality starts in the vineyard. Certain combinations of soil, climate, and cultural practices produce superior fruit. Given high-quality fruit, it is difficult for even an amateur to foul up what nature has provided.

Certain regions in the world have become known for excellent wines. These regions have a favorable combination of soil and climate and over the years have developed successful cultural methods through experience and experimentation. All these factors combine to produce world class wines.

Names like Napa, Sonoma, Livermore, Bordeaux, Burgundy, The Rheingau, and The Moselle come to mind. Although these areas are all well known in the vintner's world, wine types and styles result from a different combination of soil and climatic factors. Therefore, a given grape variety may have distinctly different characteristics in different regions.

After several thousand years of growing grapes, the Europeans have pretty well determined which varieties do best in which regions. In some well established places, growers' selections are now restricted

81

by law. For example, in Bordeaux, the French government has decreed that only grapes of the Cabernet Sauvignon family will be planted. In addition to Cabernet Sauvignon, this group includes Cabernet Franc, Merlot, Malbec, and some lesser-known varieties. In Bordeaux, white wines are made from Semillon and Sauvignon Blanc. The primary white grape in Burgundy is Chardonnay and the most important red variety is Pinot Noir. In Germany, conversely, Johannisberg Riesling, or White Riesling, is the principal premium variety. I find it interesting that we in the United States believe that the above named varieties originated in the areas named. Residents of the Rheingau, on the other hand, consider the area around the Caspian Sea to be the origin of Riesling: We're back to Noah as the Father of post-flood viticulture.

What kinds of factors do we look at in planting a vineyard to produce high-quality wine grapes? First, there is the region. Some years ago, researchers at the University of California at Davis realized that we needed a scientific system for classifying various climatic zones. Professor Winkler developed what he called a Degree Day Classification. It's based on heat summation, or the total amount of heat accumulated during a growing season. About April 1, when the vines begin to grow out of winter dormancy, high and low temperatures are recorded for the day and the average is calculated. The difference between this number and 50 degrees Fahrenheit is the heat accumulation for the day. Fifty degrees F was chosen as the base because vines come out of dormancy and start to grow at this temperature.

For example, if the high on April 1 is 80° F and the low is 56° F, the average temperature is 68° F (80 + 56 ÷ 2). Total accumulation would be 18 degree days (68 - 50 = 18).

Professor Winkler chose the period of April 1 to October 31 as the average growing period for grapes. People who use this system today sometimes start counting when the vine begins to show growth, and stop when the crop is harvested. The total number of degree days accumulated during the growing season determines the climatic region. Professor Winkler classified growing areas as follows:

Region I = 0 to 2,500 degree days
Region II = 2,501 to 3,000

Region III = 3,001 to 3,500
Region IV = 3,501 to 4,000
Region V = 4,001+

While this classification system has served the wine industry well, it has serious limitations. For example, it does not take into consideration the duration of the highs and lows. Nighttime temperatures and their duration may be very important. In the Napa Valley, the temperature often falls to 50-55°F at sunset, even after a hot summer day. In warmer areas, readings may remain above 70°F all night. As a result, many areas can be classified as Region III by the heat accumulation system but still produce Region V wines.

At about the same time, other researchers at U.C. Davis were studying grapes produced in various areas. They planted different types of vines in selected locations, made wines at the experimental winery and ranked them for quality. They found that certain varieties seemed to prefer either higher or lower heat zones. In general, the premium wine varieties did better in the cooler Regions I, II, and III. Table grapes and grapes raised for raisins, or dessert wines, in which more sugar is desirable, were better suited to the warmer climates. While this may seem quite obvious to us today, it was seen as a great step forward at the time. If the people who planted so many grapes in the late '60s and early '70s had paid more attention to the university's recommendations, they might have avoided many problems.

Yet the question of climate is more complicated than matching a grape variety to one of five regions. You may have heard the term microclimate, which literally means a small climate. Within a recognized climatic region, there may be small areas with unique conditions. For example, your vineyard might be situated off the valley in a canyon, protected from the winds. Many producers claim to benefit from a microclimate different than their neighbor's. Regretfully, unless the wines are different, and in fact better, this is pure folklore.

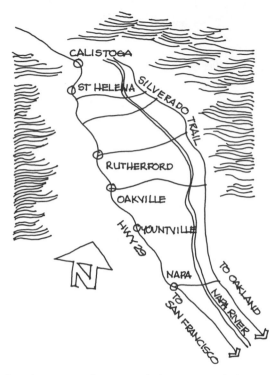

Soil is another important factor, and there are infinite combinations of soil and climate. In the Napa Valley alone, we have identified three different climatic regions. The area from Carneros, south of Napa, to somewhere near Yountville, would be classified a Region I. From Yountville to Rutherford or St. Helena is a Region II. North of St. Helena to Calistoga is a Region III. Within each one of these regions are many soil types which influence the growth of the vine and the quality of the fruit. Everytime he plants a new vineyard, a vintner or grower must match a grape variety to the climatic region and the soil type in a fashion that will produce superior fruit and wine.

I feel that Cabernet Sauvignon is consistently the best wine produced in Napa and Sonoma Counties. Nevertheless, some portions of the valley are well suited for other varieties as well. For example, in the cool Carneros Region to the south, Cabernet often has had difficulty ripening to full maturity. The use of virus-free vines may improve this to some degree.

Some people believe, correctly or not, that if the grape variety has to struggle, and if it takes the full season to ripen, it will produce the highest quality fruit and wine. Maybe that's why Cabernet Sauvignon consistently makes higher quality wine in the Napa Valley than do some of the earlier maturing varieties, such as Pinot Noir.

The French learned where to grow different kinds of grapes hundreds of years ago. That's why Pinot Noir is now produced mainly in the Burgundy region, while Cabernet Sauvignon is the grape of Bordeaux. I hope that American vintners will not need a thousand years to learn these lessons. Still, I see people planting Pinot Noir and Chardonnay next to Cabernet Sauvignon on the same soil types and in the same climatic regions. This makes no viticultural sense.

I believe that the Pinot Noir region of America is somewhere other than the Napa Valley. Our "Burgundy" area will turn out to be an area with a cooler climate, quite possibly in the coastal mountains or the regions of Monterey, Santa Maria or Anderson Valley in Mendocino County, or perhaps in Oregon or Washington.

As wine producers, we have fallen victim to what I call "the great American marketing fallacy." We believe that we must be all things to all people. It has been common to see a winery produce ten, twenty, or thirty different wines, including every generic and varietal wine you could dream of. But only one wine can be their best. Keep in mind, of course, that "best" is a subjective term. Also a producer may choose to produce the various varieties from different regions with the hope that each variety comes from the region where it excels.

I see a trend toward specialization. Many wineries are reducing the number of items they produce and concentrating on the ones they do best. I think this effort will prove beneficial to the California wine industry.

You must understand that the wine industry has many segments. Most of the white wine consumed over recent years has been produced by the larger volume wineries. In fact, most of the statistics for the wine industry are gathered from the 27 largest producers, even though there are over 700 wineries in the state. The 27 giants probably represent 90 percent of the volume. On the other hand, the most sought-after red wines tend to come from smaller operations which are geared to give more attention to barrel lots. There will always be a market for premium red wines. We hard-core bibbers will always prefer a red.

Getting back to grape-planting decisions. The grape grower still ·must choose a variety to plant in his vineyard. After looking closely at climatic conditions and soils, he might identify two or three types that could do well under a particular combination of circumstances.

There is another factor to consider. If the decision to plant grapes belongs to a winery, it simply must look at its future needs. On the other hand, if it is an independent grower who must sell his grapes to a winery, he should talk to several potential buyers. Before he plants, he must find out whether wineries have any interest in the varieties he is capable of growing. Preferably, they will give him a contract for the crop before he develops the vineyard. This practice was quite common ten years ago when it was a seller's market. In the last five-to-eight years, however, the market has been considerably softer. Wineries have been reluctant to commit themselves up front. One has to wonder if a grower should even consider planting more grapes under these circumstances. The exception might be in an area like the Napa Valley, where there is an Agricultural Preserve requiring a 40-acre minimum parcel size, and where wine grapes have been shown to be the best use of the land. Unfortunately, there still may or may not be a return on investment in a new Napa Valley vineyard today, since law requires land must remain in agriculture, all other options have been taken away from owners. I would venture to say that legislation which results in the creation of an agricultural preserve, while attractive in principle, has variously reduced the price of grapes and inflated the price of land till it makes little economic sense.

Let's assume, however, that planting a vineyard does make economic sense. A grower has studied both climate and soil, and has made the decision to proceed. If the ground has been fallow or planted to some other crop in the past, he probably would have the field ripped to a depth of three feet to break up any substructures and allow for good root penetration by vines. If there have been trees on the property, such as oaks or prunes, he might fumigate the parcel (or at least in the area where the trees were located) with some chemical to kill fungus.

If the ground has been previously planted to grapevines, there is a distinct chance that it is infested with critters that could bring the future vineyard to a short and unprofitable end. One of the most dangerous pests is the wormlike nematode which feeds on the roots of grapevines. Some species can weaken the vines, and others transmit virus. Nematodes can reduce grape production and cause the vineyard to be unprofitable.

Phylloxera, or root louse, to which we have already referred, also feeds on the roots of grapevines. Phylloxera is deadly to Vinifera. Grape growers plant an American grapevine and then graft or bud a Vinifera variety above the rooted portion. Thus everything below the ground is American and everything above the ground, referred to as the "scion," is a European variety. This is common practice today.

The following spring the grapevine begins to grow. As a member of the vine family, it has a natural tendency to climb, so a wood or metal grapestake is provided to support it. That first year, the grower will tie the young grapevine to a stake to make sure the trunk is straight and strong. He prunes selectively, cutting off shoots in locations where they are not desired so that the remaining ones will have more strength. This practice is commonly referred to as "suckering."

Most modern vineyards have trellis systems, consisting of wires strung parallel to and at least 36 inches above the ground. The exact

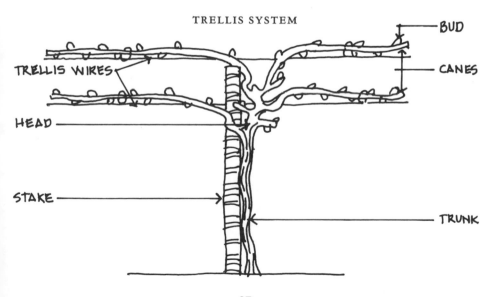

TRELLIS SYSTEM

height at which trellis wires are placed is related to springtime frost and methods of harvest. (I will describe frost-protection strategies later.) Trellis wires support the horizontal growth of vines once they have reached a desired height. The wires also help spread the grapevines out so that more leaves are exposed to the sun. As I've already mentioned, it's the leaves that produce the sugar and acid for the fruit. Spreading them makes the plant more efficient.

Various methods are used to train grapevines. In modern viticulture, the most common are cane and cordon. If you are interested in growing grapevines, I recommend that you read Professor A.J. Winkler's book, *General Viticulture,* or contact your local farm advisor. In addition, the University of California Extension Service, Berkeley, has published excellent pamphlets on training and pruning grapevines.

Once a vine has been trained, it is important to establish a proper pruning level. This is done during winter, when vines are dormant. Pruning determines the amount of crop on the vine. To maximize profit, a grower wants to maximize crops. Yet he must be careful to avoid "overcropping." It is possible to leave so much fruit on the vine that a plant is incapable of producing the proper sugar/acid ratio, color, aroma and flavor. The result is poor grape quality.

Over a number of years, a grower can experiment with various vines, leaving more or less wood or brush on vines at pruning. At various pruning levels he can track the quality of the fruit, measured by sugar/acid ratio, color, and crop size.

A grape plant normally reaches full maturity in five to eight years. From that point until it is 40 to 60 years old, it will produce what we call a "full crop." An experienced pruner can look at a dormant vine and tell from the vigor of canes that grew the previous year whether or not it was pruned properly. If the vine was cut back too severely, he will see extreme vigor because only a few buds would have been left to grow. Although the vine was healthy, the crop was reduced. If it shows poor growth, too many buds may have been left during the last pruning season. Such a plant carried an excessive load during the summer growing season, resulting in poor quality fruit and poor growth.

When springtime comes, and average daytime temperatures reach 50° F, juices start to flow and the vine begins to grow. This is a crucial time. From mid-March on, as the vines begin to grow, nighttime temperatures can still drop below 32° F. If the vines are frosted, an entire crop can be lost. Later, vines will re-grow and by the middle of summer, they may look perfectly normal to the untrained eye. But there will be little or no fruit on the regrowth—a disaster for the grape grower. Thus, considerable time and money are spent trying to protect a crop from spring frost. Although the danger period is probably over by May 1, it has always been my practice to have the vineyard manager leave his frost alarm on until June 1. Freak freezes have been known in May.

The frost sensor is a device called a thermistor. Because cold tends to settle in low spots, the grower places thermistors in the lowest parts of his vineyard. They can be set for any temperature. For frost warnings, 33° to 34° F are common. When the temperature around the thermistor reaches this level, an alarm sounds in the grower's bedroom. He goes out to check field thermometers and to decide whether to turn on his frost protection.

Wind machines are a traditional and relatively inefficient means of frost protection. If you have driven through the wine country, you have probably seen giant propellers, 10 to 30 feet high, out in the middle of the vineyard. These propellers mix the warm air above the vineyard with cold air near the ground. Depending on the conditions, this can sometimes keep the air close to the vines at or above 32° F.

If the temperature continues to fall, the grower may ignite oil heaters around the vineyard. The wind machine mixes hot air from the heaters with cold air in the vineyard. This method of frost protection will protect a vineyard until the temperature outside the protected area reaches 27° or 28° F. Burning diesel oil creates a pollution problem, although some of the better heaters burn the fuel more efficiently and create less pollution than do automobiles. This method also requires the grower and his helpers to work eight hours or more during the night, tending heaters and wind machines. Then they have to spend the next day refueling the machinery.

Irrigation is a more modern and more efficient method of frost protection. There is a striking irony: it turns out that you can protect

89

a vine from frost by coating it with ice. I often wonder who first discovered this, since most of us tend to associate ice with frost.

While water freezes at 32° F, grapevines are not damaged until they are cooled to 31° F for one-half hour. If you coat the vine with ice and maintain its temperature at 32° F, you can actually insulate the new growth from the cold air. Of course, you must make sure that the ice's temperature does not fall to that of the outside air. So you continue to spray the vines as long as the temperature remains below freezing. New ice is continually formed at 32° F, giving up heat in the process and keeping the vine at that level. This method assumes, of course, that springtime temperatures will not fall below 24° F. Nevertheless, irrigation is 4 degrees more effective than wind machines and heaters.

Water is applied lightly. If too much ice forms, the weight can break off young shoots. This would be as disastrous as frost itself. We apply a tenth of an inch per-hour. Many nights, the outside temperature does not drop far enough to form ice, yet when a grower's entire yearly income is out there in that cold night, he has a tendency to turn the sprinklers on at 33° or 34° F. This costs him only some sleep and the power required to run the system. He also starts the sprinklers early because when the water is first applied, the air temperature falls briefly before stabilizing.

Sprinkling for frost protection requires a great amount of water— approximately 50 gallons per minute per acre. A 250-acre vineyard needs 750,000 gallons of water for each hour of frost protection. It takes six diesel engines to pump that quantity. There are no wells in the North Coast that will support such a volume. Therefore, many growers build 30- to 40-million-gallon reservoirs to hold a three-day frost protection water supply. While the grower is frost protecting, he also pumps water from his well into the reservoir day and night. If he has to deal with three or four eight-hour frigid nights in a row, he will still have some water by the last night. This much need for frost protection is most unusual, but many Napa Valley growers remember 1970, when they had to protect against frost 35 nights in a row.

Frost is a frightening prospect. Although your entire income for a year is at risk, it always strikes me that it creates a great social hour for the grape grower. Everyone is up in the dark—sometimes at

9 P.M. sometimes at midnight, sometimes at 4 A.M.—and once you are up you might as well stay up until sunrise. After all, it is not until then that the temperature begins to rise, and once you start your sprinklers and coat the vines with ice, you have to keep spraying until it melts.

On a frigid night, you will find groups of two or three pickup trucks parked where property lines meet. Your neighbors will be discussing everything from the temperature and the price of grapes to local politics. You can always rely on some growers to panic and turn on their frost protection hours before it is needed. Old-timers will continue to check their thermometers and often will not start their frost protection even after most of their neighbors have already initiated spraying. Some people wait too long and suffer some frost damage because they do not start their system. By mid-morning their frosted vines will wilt. Within a day or two, blackened frost pockets will appear in the vineyard. They become the laughing stock of the local coffee shop for waiting too long to turn on their protection.

I often wonder if we will ever have a serious frost in the Napa Valley again. There is so much frost protection in the Valley now that when the frost alarm goes off and the protection starts, the entire microclimate changes immediately. It is possible that the small number of growers who do not have frost protection, and who take their chances every year, will never again suffer damage from cold. If they escape the frost, they come out way ahead, because protection is terribly expensive. Since everyone gets the same price for grapes, those who have not paid for a system of defense enjoy a substantially higher return on investment than those who do. Of course, if a serious frost comes, a system will pay for itself in one night.

When the soil begins to dry out in the spring, the grower cultivates as soon as the ground is dry enough to support a tractor. Because clean, cultivated ground holds the daytime heat better than weed-covered ground, it reduces the chance of frost in a vineyard. Also, weeds compete with vines for soil moisture. The better wine-grape growing regions usually need no irrigation, so the grower does not want weeds to compete with his vines for natural moisture.

As the vine grows during the spring and summer, it is threatened by a whole new set of problems. For example, there is Pierce Disease, transported by the Sharpshooter Leaf Hopper. This insect survives

91

winter in the vegetation along river and creek banks only to feed on grapevines during the growing season. If it infects a vine, the plant will die.

The vine attracts other insects, including mites, cutworms and the common grape leaf hopper. All of them feed on the leaves. Remember that the leaf must remain whole, green and healthy in order to produce sugar and acid efficiently. Anything that affects the health and color of these leaves, whether it be insects, lack of moisture, or viruses that turn the vineyards red and yellow in the fall, inhibits fruit maturation and quality.

Powdery mildew and a fungus called Botrytis are also common in California vineyards. If mildew or Botrytis grow on grape clusters, a winery may reject the fruit. The reason mildew is so undesirable is that its unpleasant flavor and aroma spoil wine.

On the other hand, Botrytis is acceptable and even encouraged in certain varieties of grapes and wine, under some conditions. Botrytis is the organism responsible for the late-harvest Riesling character, the Trokenbeerenauslese of Germany, and the Sauternes of France. But in most red wines and many whites, this character is considered a defect to be eliminated by fungicide sprays.

In the springtime when grape flowers are in bloom, the grower may collect a random sample of the leaf stems, called petioles. By having the petioles analyzed in a laboratory, he can determine the fertilizer needs of his grapevines. Because the plants can put down root systems 30 feet deep, they usually need no fertilization.

When a grapevine does require fertilization, it is very specific in its needs. If a vine needs potassium, for example, you are wasting your money on a fertilizer that combines nitrogen, potassium, and some other element. For this reason, I question the value of combination fertilizers. Carbon, hydrogen, oxygen, potassium, phosphorus and nitrogen are essential because they are all involved in either sugar or amino acid production. But if a grower fertilizes indiscriminately, excess nitrogen, for instance, can be a problem. It causes rapid growth which may result in "shatter." Shatter can occur if the vine is growing too rapidly while the grape flowers are being pollinated, resulting in a low percentage of flowers turning into berries. This is referred to as a "poor set." A "good set," on the other hand, means that a high percentage of the flowers were pollinated, producing clusters with many berries and a good crop.

Because the flowers of most grape varieties contain both male and female elements, cross-pollination, or the use of bees, is not as important as it is with some fruit trees. The biggest enemy of good set is weather. Just talk to a farmer; you usually learn that the weather is too hot, too cold, too wet, too dry, or too windy.

Average annual rainfall is critical as well. In the Napa Valley it is 33 inches. Most of the rain comes between November 1 and May 1. Rarely will we have rain during the summer and fall. One of the problems encountered by growers in other states is that they get summer and fall rains. An untimely rain can lead to rot problems in grape clusters, degrading the resulting wine.

Another problem in some states is extremely low winter temperatures. All varieties of the species Vinifera are vulnerable to temperatures below 0° F, even when they are dormant. In New York and Washington, for example, growers have suffered substantial losses through winter kill. This is not a problem in California. In fact, winter temperatures rarely drop below 20° F in the grape-growing regions of the state.

With 33 inches of rainfall during the winter, and 30-foot root systems, mature vines can get through the growing season without any supplemental water. Irrigation systems which are used primarily for frost protection can also be used for cooling on hot summer days. Many growers turn on the sprinklers if the temperature goes above 95° F. The spray of water protects the fruit from sunburn. The same sprinklers can also be used for frost protection in the fall. If the vines are still growing and succulent, an early frost can kill the wood and the buds you plan to leave for next year's crop. Growers may choose to frost protect during the first few cold fall nights, giving the vines a chance to "harden." The wood turns from green to brown and the plant prepares to withstand the winter cold.

It is a common misconception that irrigated vineyards produce lower quality grapes than non-irrigated vineyards. Even in the premium wine-grape growing regions, you will find irrigated vineyards. Some people in the wine business don't like to talk about this, but they really need not apologize. It's a matter of common sense.

They know that if the vine finds enough natural moisture in the soil to sustain it, then, of course, additional irrigation will simply pump too much water into the fruit. The berries will grow larger, but sugar, acidity, and flavor will be diluted. On the other hand, during drought years, the vines want something to drink. This was true in the 1976 and 1977 seasons.

Some of the older literature indicates that superior wines are produced in drought years, yet I think most wine judges rank 1976 as a mediocre vintage in the Napa Valley, and 1977 as quite good. We only had 11 inches of rain, one-third of normal, during each of these years. I can't explain why one was better than the other or why wines made in these two years were so different. Obviously, rainfall is not the sole factor. I know for a fact that the people who did not have supplemental irrigation in 1976 and 1977 harvested a much lighter crop, of no better quality than did those who were able to give their vines a drink.

Another popular myth is the belief that if a vine produces a smaller crop the quality will be higher. If I see a Cabernet vineyard consistently producing two tons to the acre, or half a normal crop, I might conclude that the vines have some serious problems. They could simply be old. More likely, they could be affected by a virus or poor soil. Some people believe that vines infected with viruses might produce grapes with some special attributes; however, I know from experience that virus-free vines produce larger crops with better sugar, better acidity, better color.

It is always tempting to rationalize a position. If someone has an old vineyard that does not produce a normal crop, he might convince himself that the quality is higher. Granted, overcropping can be a problem, but a low-yielding vineyard does not necessarily produce high-quality grapes. Plus, research has shown that thinning a crop does not guarantee better wine.

To say that a virus-sickened grapevine, producing half a crop, produces better grapes than a healthy grapevine, is nonsense, and would be better applied to the sick vineyard than promulgated as P.R.

When I host tastings of my wines, people frequently ask: "How old are the vines these wines came from?" It's irrelevant. The real question is: "Do you like the wine or don't you?" I suspect that people with old vineyards have promoted the notion that wine quality is somehow related to the age of the vine. I call this backing into a marketing strategy. When a vine is two to three years old, it may produce one-eighth to one-quarter of a normal crop. The next year, production might increase to a quarter or a third of par. Possibly by the sixth or eighth year, the vine is bearing a full crop. If it doesn't have other problems, the mature vine can produce a full crop each year for the next 40 years or so. (A full crop must be defined in relation to the variety, the soil type, the trellis system, and other specific vineyard conditions).

At a certain point, like all of us, the vine begins to slow down. As tonnage declines each year, the grower must decide whether it is more economical to tear out that old vineyard and replant it or to let it produce a little longer on a declining basis. Even vineyards are subject to the law of diminishing returns.

A mature vineyard, from 8 to 40 years old, usually produces grapes of more consistent quality than a young vineyard. Nevertheless, it has been my experience that, on a young vine, the grapes may mature earlier in the season, have more sugar, more acidity, and lower pH. All of these factors contribute to high quality wine. I have seen vineyards that looked good in their first six years, but produced disappointing wines when they hit maximum production age. So I disagree with the maxim that older vines produce better quality wine. More consistent wine, possibly. But better quality? Not necessarily.

By the time the vine has shown six inches of shoot growth in the springtime, the grower begins to apply elemental sulfur to prevent the growth of powdery mildew. He starts early in the season because elemental sulfur will only prevent mildew before the infestation appears. He must literally cover the new growth with sulfur to prevent the mildew from getting started. He again applies sulfur with each additional six inches of new growth. This may involve dusting every two to three weeks. Depending on location and growing conditions, growers dust as rarely as twice a year or as frequently as ten times or more.

If the mildew does get started, treatment is quite costly. It requires mixing sulfur with 300 to 500 gallons of water per acre and then literally soaking the vines and the clusters. The water actually eliminates the mildew, while the wetable sulfur stays on as a preventative and replaces one dusting operation. Why not simply turn on the sprinklers and apply 500 gallons of water per acre, inject wetable sulfur in the water supply, or dust later with a helicopter? Unfortunately, these strategies do not work. You need sprayers blowing the water under tremendous pressure, so that it penetrates into the clusters and all parts of the vine.

Sometime during the season, the grower must cut off his dusting program and allow sulfur to dissipate; otherwise, elemental sulfur will be carried with the grapes into the winery. During fermentation, sulfur will combine with hydrogen to produce hydrogen sulfide, which smells like rotten eggs. Obviously, this odor is highly undesirable in any wine. Most wineries encourage their growers to stop their sulfuring some six weeks before anticipated harvest dates. By the time the grapes reach the stage we call "veraison"—the time when white grapes begin to change from hard green to yellow green, and red grapes from green to red—they have enough sugar content to prevent mildew. If the grapes develop from 11 to 13 percent sugar and are clean of mildew, they should not require further sulfur.

Now comes the quietest part of the growing season. The grower really has nothing to do but wait for the grapes to reach proper sugar levels. He tests them frequently to monitor their maturity.

In days past, sugar was considered the primary, if not the only, measure of maturity. Remember that sugar is converted by a specific chemical reaction into ethyl alcohol. If the vintner has determined what percent alcohol he wants in each variety, he can calculate the percent sugar at which he wants the grapes delivered.

The chemical formula for fermentation, put most simply, is:

$$\text{Sugar} \xrightarrow{\text{YEAST}} \text{Ethyl Alcohol} + \text{Carbon Dioxide}$$

Approximately 56 percent of the sugar is converted into ethyl alcohol. For example, Cabernet Sauvignon grapes, with a sugar content of 23.0 percent, will produce wines of 12.8 to 12.9 alcohol (23.0 × .56 = 12.88). In practice, the alcohol level often does not come out exactly as predicted. There can be several explanations for discrepancies. A sugar test might not have been accurate. Or the conversion of sugar to alcohol might not have been completely efficient. Inefficient conversion could be related to the strain of yeast or to the availability of yeast nutrients in grape juice. Recent studies indicate that summer growing conditions can also affect alcoholic conversions.

It is important to know how to take an accurate sugar test in the vineyard. Several weeks before an anticipated harvest date, the vintner or his manager should walk through the vineyard and take a grape sample. There is an old saying that the best treatment for a vineyard is the footprint of the grower. One who walks through his fields frequently and cares for it tends to produce better-quality grapes. Four-wheel motorcycles have been a boon to vineyardists. Perhaps the footprint of a four-wheeler is also a good treatment. But walking is indispensible for taking a good grape sample. The more rows you cover, the more likely you are to gather an accurate sample. A given vineyard may have several different soil types, which affect the variety and its maturity. Grapes on one side of the vine will mature faster than those on the other side simply because they are more exposed to the sun. Frequently vine rows are laid out east-to-west so that in summer the sun's path is parallel to the vine row. North-and-south rows tend to sunburn more on the west side where they face the afternoon sun. On the other hand, in the northern hemisphere, fruit hanging on the south side of vines are generally riper than fruit on the north. To take an accurate sample then, a grower must walk through as much of the vineyard as possible, picking berries randomly from both sides of the vine.

It doesn't seem to matter whether the sample is picked in whole clusters or in single berries. If you sample whole clusters, you need buckets full of grapes to obtain an accurate sample. I generally walk through a vineyard with a small plastic sandwich bag in my hand, taking berries here and there, until I have a minimum of a hundred or have covered most of the vineyard.

When I was a grape buyer for a large winery, we used to calculate bonuses and penalties based on sugar content. Frequently the growers wanted me to take the samples and tell them when to harvest. They would become upset if they brought in their grapes and did not receive a bonus for high sugar. So I would usually cover myself by taking most of the sample off the north sides of the vines, knowing that they would be greener. When the north side was near the desired maturity, I could be fairly certain that the sugar test at the winery would read higher than my field sample.

Once a sample is gathered, I first crush the grapes in a beaker. An instrument called a refractometer is used to determine the sugar content of the juice. As its name indicates, this device measures the refraction of light. If you have a temperature-compensated refractometer, simply pour a little juice on it, look into the eyepiece as though it were a telescope, and read the sugar content on the scale. Non-temperature-compensated refractometers are submerged into the juice until the temperature equalizes.

It's a good idea to start taking weekly samples three weeks before the anticipated harvest date and to sample even more frequently as you get close to the desired sugar level. Grapes, when harvested, should arrive at the winery very close to their target sugar content.

To determine maturity today, vintners are looking at other criteria in addition to sugar content. Sugar/acid ratio is important. Vintners are also paying more attention to pH, which is particularly important in the longevity of a red wine. The color of the fruit and the condition of the vine are other determining factors. There are times when grapes are not as high in sugar as you might like. Yet, looking at the vine, you see that it is tired and does not have any more energy to put into the cluster. You might as well pick the fruit rather than wait for more sugar and watch the vine go downhill.

If the variety has been properly matched to the climatic and soil conditions, the four biggest culprits causing late maturity are the weather, virus, overcropping, and poor culture. The grower cannot control the weather but planting virus-free vines is advisable. The grower can prune properly or take other steps to control the crop level, so that too much fruit will not prevent the crop from reaching full maturity. Finally, if he has not cultivated the weeds and controlled insects, it is likely that grapes will never reach proper maturity.

I know there is much concern about insecticides these days. In my view, the grower who uses the most insecticides usually has the most insect problems because if you start a consistent spraying program, you also kill natural predators. On the other hand, if a vineyard is invaded by some type of insect that is going to harm the vines, I think that insecticides should be applied. Like any other technology, insecticides must be used rationally. It is essential to follow label regulations, which include application rates and dates to cut off application before harvest.

We have now reached the culmination of a grower's year. Excitement fills the air and much work needs to be done. It is time to gather the crop from the vines.

God loves fermentation just as
dearly as he does vegetation.
RALPH WALDO EMERSON
1803-1882

8.
Fermentation

We've already alluded to the fermentation equation but in this chapter we'll discuss the process in more detail, since it is the key to wine production. I have heard it said that vintners are simply babysitting Mother Nature because, in reality, we are manipulating microorganisms either to bring about beneficial effects or to prevent undesirable changes.

When I tell people I have a Master's Degree in grape growing and winemaking, they often look puzzled, intimating that it should not take years of study to learn how to drink wine after stomping grapes with your bare feet. If that was all we'd done in college, it would've been a lot more fun. Actually, the winemaking curriculum is very heavily devoted to chemistry, biochemistry, and microbiology. If the vintner uses correct yeast and bacteria, and knows how to control them, winemaking can be rather simple, and the vintner can take credit only for not having goofed up. But, of course, even simple things have a way of becoming complicated sometimes. Take fermentation, for example. It can variously be defined as: (1) agitation (2) seething or (3) the conversion by microorganisms of one organic substance to another.

100

Complicating matters even further, in the production of wine, we speak of primary and secondary fermentations. Primary fermentation is the conversion of sugar by yeast to ethyl alcohol and carbon dioxide gas. We also talk about secondary fermentations, which are bacterial conversions. The first is malolactic fermentation: the conversion by bacteria of malic acid to lactic acid. This change is considered desirable in some wines but not in others. The second is the conversion of ethyl alcohol by bacteria to acetic acid or vinegar. This effect is always considered undesirable, so the vintner should take precautions to prevent it.

As shown in the previous chapter, the fermentation equation can be depicted quite simply:

$$\text{Sugar} \xrightarrow{\text{YEAST}} \text{Ethyl Alcohol} + \text{Carbon Dioxide}$$

Following this, we should understand, up front, that what we want to accomplish in alcoholic fermentation is quite different from what the yeast cell wants to accomplish. The yeast cell, given sugar as a nutrient source and all the oxygen it would like, will simply use the sugar as a food to produce huge amounts of new cells, with water and carbon dioxide as by-products. Generally, oxygen is available early in the fermentation, simply because it is impossible not to pick up some in the crushing of the grapes and the pumping of the "must," a term used to describe the combination of juice, skins and seeds from the crush. Also, sulfur dioxide might have been added to the "must" to inhibit any wild yeast which might have come on the fruit, since it sticks to the "bloom," a waxy substance on the outside of the grape skins. Vintners inhibit the wild yeast by adding sulfur dioxide because they don't know whether these have the capability of completing fermentation in a rapid and efficient manner. Instead, they prefer to use cultured yeasts *(Saccharomyces cerevisiae)*. Two common cultured yeast strains used in California are the champagne strain and the montrachet strain. These are tolerant to sulfur dioxide and have a good track record for effecting clean and complete fermentations. Years ago it was necessary for wineries, commercial laboratories, or universities to culture the yeast strain on a growth media year round, so that it would be available when needed. Today vintners can buy dehydrated yeast much as a baker does, so that when added to warm water for a short period of time, it will be ready to function.

Although vintners don't add oxygen to the "must," they don't make any attempt to eliminate it, because a certain amount is necessary for the rapid proliferation of yeast cells. When oxygen is available to the cells, they will propogate rapidly and produce by-products of water and carbon dioxide gas. When there is no longer oxygen available, fermentation will be anaerobic and yeast will begin to convert the sugar to ethyl alcohol and carbon dioxide gas. While the efficiency of conversion will depend on some of the factors mentioned in the last chapter, 56 percent by volume is a good working figure. This means that if a vintner decided that his white table wine tasted best at 11.2 percent alcohol by volume, he would attempt to pick the grapes at 20.0 percent sugar (11.2 ÷ .56 = 20.0).

What about the temperature of fermentation? It's important to the aromas and flavors of the final product; therefore, fermentation tanks with cooling jackets are used so that the temperature can be controlled. In general, a cooler fermentation will be slower and will maintain more of the fruity, varietal character of the grape. Aroma components, on the other hand, are very volatile and can be driven off by heat. Also, the fermentation temperature could contribute to the diversion of sugar to products other than ethyl alcohol, products such as glycerol, lactic acid, diacetyl, acetaldehyde, as well as higher alcohols like butanol. The production of all these side products is also a function of the yeast strain and bacteria present in the fermentation.

It's natural for high-energy compounds, such as sugars, to convert to lower-energy compounds. This is exactly the case in fermentation: sugar, through the action of microorganisms, will be converted to ethyl alcohol and carbon dioxide gas and if care is not taken, a bacteria can further convert ethyl alcohol to acetic acid. Vintners must control or stop this last natural conversion.

When we speak of "dry wines," we are referring to what happens when the yeast is allowed to run its course and convert all fermentable sugars to ethyl alcohol and carbon dioxide gas, thus reducing or eliminating sweetness. If a vintner wishes to produce a wine with some residual sweetness from unfermented grape sugar which remains in the wine, he must stop the yeast from completing the fermentation. This is usually accomplished through a combination of practices: First, he might lower the fermentation temperature, because cooler temperatures will slow down any chemical reaction. If the temperature is low enough, fermentation comes to a virtual standstill. The wine might then be filtered or centrifuged in order to remove all or as many yeast cells as possible. A slight addition of sulfur dioxide will further inhibit the action of any remaining yeast. Through a combination of practices such as these, vintners can produce wines with a slight savor of natural grape sugar, such as some of the pleasant Chenin Blancs and Johannisberg Rieslings you might have tasted.

However, making natural sweet wines is roughly equivalent to sitting on a dynamite keg. Since nature has not made the transformation from high energy to low energy complete, it is generally necessary to keep these wines refrigerated until they are to be bottled, at which time it is required that they be sterile-filtered through a membrane of a pore size that yeast and bacteria cannot pass. The bottles into which the product is put must be meticulously clean and even the filling and corking machine have to be carefully sterilized and monitored to make sure they are not a source of yeast infection, which could cause the wine to complete its fermentation in the bottle. That process, in turn, could be the cause of sediment or cloudiness but, more importantly, it can create pressure from the carbon dioxide it produces. In such a style of wine, gasiness may not be considered a defect; however, internal pressure can become so great that it will push the cork out or even blow up the bottle! Sediment and cloudiness are certainly undesirable, but not explosive.

Other winemaking products in which yeast plays an important role are Champagne and Sherry, which I'll discuss in later chapters. I'll pass over bread, other baker products, and beer entirely.

The first bacterial conversion in winemaking is the conversion of malic into lactic acid by the activity of lactic acid bacteria. As I've said, this is considered undesirable in some wines, but not in others. As a general guideline, understand first that lactic acid is a weaker or softer acid than malic; therefore, when the vintner wishes to reduce acidity, malolactic fermentation is desirable. In a cooler growing region, where the respiration of acid in grapes is low because of cool temperatures, malolactic fermentation in wine would be most desirable. This is not the case in a warmer climate where some of the acidity has been lost from grapes through respiration in the vineyard. In addition, the bouquet of some wines is affected for the better by malolactic fermentation. Consequently, such a fermentation in a red wine may be considered desirable because it makes the bouquet more complex; in a white wine, however, it may be undesirable as it detracts from the forward, fruity character. Some winemakers go so far as to cause one portion of a given wine to go through a malolactic fermentation, and to prevent the other portion from doing so, and finish later by blending the two parts together.

If the malolactic fermentation is desired, it is currently common practice to inoculate grape juice with lactic-acid bacteria at the same time that the yeast culture is added. In the past this was not done because that particular bacteria can also use sugar as an energy source; it has been determined that the amount of sugar used is very small and, besides yeast will convert sugar to ethyl alcohol much quicker than the bacteria can convert it to lactic acid.

Containers used for fermentation also make a difference. If a vintner ferments in stainless-steel tanks, malolactic fermentation should not develop unless, of course, bacteria has been introduced. On the other hand, if wood fermenters which have been used before are re-used, whether they are larger tanks or small barrels, it may be impossible to prevent malolactic fermentation. To prevent it, it would be necessary to employ the same practices mentioned earlier for stopping yeast action: Centrifuging, filtering, lowering the temperature, or adding sulfur dioxide. These practices could, however, stop the yeast fermentation. Therefore, stainless steel fermenters, because they have cooling jackets and can be sterilized, are the vessels most commonly used today.

If a vintner chooses to do barrel fermentations of white wines such as Chardonnay or Fumé Blanc, and he does not desire malolactic fermentation, new barrels are necessary each season.

Malolactic transformation is an anaerobic process. Since it does not require oxygen, it can occur concurrently with the yeast conversion. Keeping the barrels or tanks full after fermentation will not prevent the anaerobic process. Such is not the case with acetobacter, which produces vinegar, which we will discuss in a bit.

The vintner may want to prevent the wine from undergoing the malolactic process. While the wine is in the bulk stage during aging, not only will the centrifuge or filter be used along with cool temperatures and sulfur dioxide gas, but it is also necessary to take the same care in bottling that would be taken in bottling a white wine with residual sugar. This is why I often tell people that a person doesn't have to be too bright if he only makes Cabernet Sauvignon at his winery, as I do. Once the red wine is dry and gone through malolactic, it is microbiologically stable. Extreme cautions are not necessary before bottling.

Lactic acid bacteria and the production of lactic acid are important in the development of other food products that you might enjoy, such as sauerkraut, pickles, cheese, sour cream, buttermilk, yogurt, sourdough french bread, olives, some sausages, soy sauce, sake, and something called Bantu Beer. Also "sour mash" whiskey derives some of its unique character from the fact that the beer produced for the distillation also undergoes a malolactic fermentation. Lactic acid also provides the tartness of sour milk, and many products called "sour."

Before closing this chapter, I'd like to talk about the conversion of ethyl alcohol to acetic acid (vinegar) by acetobacter. Remember the saying that years ago wine was "something like grape juice in December and something like vinegar in June"? It will make sense to you if you understand that before acetobacter was better understood as a microorganism requiring oxygen to function, it was the biggest single factor in the spoilage of wines. In one of his lectures describing the difficulties in winemaking before microbiology was better understood, Dr. Amerine said something to the effect that, by Christmas each year, 25 percent of the year's wines were spoiled and that by a year later only 25 percent of the total were still good.

Pasteur's discovery that acetobacter required oxygen, and that it was responsible for the production of vinegar, was a great advance in quality control. The most simple prevention is to keep the containers full so that there is no air space. In professional winemaking, a vintner will have many sizes of containers so that if necessary to pump a wine from a larger tank, a combination of smaller tanks which will be totally filled by the wine can be employed. Smaller containers, from half-gallons to fifty-gallon barrels, are also available for the regular topping of the wine, since evaporation and leakage during aging create head-space. It is this head-space that makes vinegar production possible. On the home-winemaking level, it is possible to use for topping purposes smaller bottles that can be filled with wine. If such bottles are not available, or only a barrel or less of wine is made, people sometimes boil stones to clean and sterilize them, then fill the container—topping it off—by simply dropping them in.

Now that you understand that lack of head space and the judicious use of sulfur dioxide will prevent the functioning of acetobacter, it may not seem so great a problem, but when you think about the fact that commercial vinegar can be made almost instantly by running wine or apple cider through a container saturated with acetobacter and oxygen, it gets scary. I prefer a bottle of good red wine. Unfortunately, I've opened bottles with wine labels on them to find them more ready for the salad bowl than the wine glass.

I've made the statement that, naturally, a high-energy compound, such as sugar, wants to proceed to a lower-energy state. I used the example of stopping the fermentation short to make a naturally sweet wine. You can see from the previous discussion that it is also natural for yeast to convert sugar to ethyl alochol and equally natural for acetobacter to convert the ethyl alcohol to vinegar. While the vintner may choose to produce a dry or naturally sweet wine and use appropriate methods, it is never desirable in winemaking to produce vinegar, so every precaution is utilized to stop nature from proceeding further once ethyl alcohol is produced.

If you didn't know how vinegar was produced before, I hope you understand now. As a footnote, I might add that when you buy commercially produced vinegar with no specific description, you can generally assume that it is made by fermenting apple juice to apple cider, then converting the ethyl alcohol to acetic acid. On the other hand, if wine is the base, it is generally labeled "Wine Vinegar."

Wine is like sex in that few
men will admit not knowing
all about it.

HUGH JOHNSON, 1882-1942

9.
Production of Table Wine

Harvest time arrives when the vintner determines by field sampling that the grapes are ripe. Ripeness is a subjective term. It depends on the amount of alcohol you want in your wine and whether you want the wine to be dry or to retain some sugar. In general, white grapes might be harvested at 20 to 23 degrees Brix (or percent sugar), and red grapes at 21 to 24 degrees Brix.

Vintners also must decide whether to harvest by hand or machine. A mechanical harvester looks like a lumber carrier or a car wash on wheels. As the machine straddles a row, various striker mechanisms shake the vines or trellis wires. Individual grapes and clusters rain down on conveyor belts and are carried out to a gondola. In my opinion, machine harvesting is most suitable for red wines because mechanical harvesters frequently break up clusters and partially crush the fruit. Remember that the juice of both red and white grapes is without color. The difference is in the skins. All the pigments that color red wines are in the skin. To make a red, you ferment skins and juice together. That's why mechanical harvesting, which may cause a lot of juicing in the grape gondolas is not a problem for red wines. You want skin/juice contact anyway.

On the other hand, mechanical harvest can be detrimental for white varieties. If the machine breaks a lot of berries, the juice may be damaged by oxidation, enzymatic browning, and premature fermentation. Some vintners machine-harvest white varieties, but they use presses or crushers in the field so that the skins can be separated from the juice as soon as possible. We'll later discuss occasions on which some period of skin contact for some white varieties is desirable.

The advantage of the mechanical harvester is that it can do the work of 20 to 40 pickers. This makes it possible to harvest quantities of grapes quickly at optimum maturity. Also, the harvester can be equipped with lights to work during the night, when temperatures may be 20° to 40°F. lower than in the heat of the day. Cooler juice temperatures can be a positive quality factor. Last, and perhaps best, mechanical harvesters never threaten to go on strike at the last minute before harvest.

Once grapes are harvested, whether white or red, it is important to get them to the winery as quickly as possible. They are weighed, either in the field or at the winery for the purpose of paying the pickers or the grower. If they are the winery's own grapes, the vintner needs to track the number of gallons per-ton to make sure his presses and other equipment are operating efficiently.

At the same time, a sample of the grapes is analyzed in the laboratory for sugar, total acidity, and pH. Some wineries may analyze for other factors but these three are the most important indicators of quality. Most wineries that buy grapes from independent growers have bonus and penalty systems based on the sugar content of the grapes. Some pay according to sugar, acid, pH, and color, or any combination of these factors.

To inhibit wild yeast, enzymatic browning, and oxidation, sulfur dioxide in some form may be added to the grape juice in the field or at the winery. Modern wineries all use special yeast cultures to ferment the grapes. I suppose that vintners of ancient times were forced to depend on good luck or superstition rather than scientific methods. Perhaps some old, established European wineries still depend on wild yeast that comes in with the grapes. While this is romantic, I doubt that many wineries actually gamble on unknown yeast cultures because the wrong one could ruin a lot of expensive juice. Today, vintners grow their own yeast cultures from known strains or they use commercially available dehydrated strains which tolerate alcohol, ferment all sugar in the juice, and produce favorable aromas and flavors. These commercial cultures are tolerant to low-levels of sulfur dioxide, so treating grapes with SO_2 inhibits only wild yeast, not the cultured strain.

Grapes next go through a stemmer/crusher. This machine separates stems from fruit and breaks up the berries; stems are then discarded and you are left with "must," a term used to describe the combination of juice, skins and seeds.

If the desired end-product is a high-quality sparkling wine, some vintners do not even use a stemmer/crusher. They put the grape clusters directly into a press and extract the juice with as little skin contact as possible. A few producers of white table wine use the same method.

Another new technique is the use of chillers to bring down the temperature of the "must." This prevents, or slows down, undesirable processes such as premature fermentation, enzymatic browning, and oxidation. Research and experience have demonstrated that clean, cool juice produces wines with more favorable aromas, while juices retaining a high percentage of solids have a tendency to produce more undesirable flavors and aromas.

WHITE WINE

Up to this point, both red and white grapes are handled similarly. Now the road divides. Depending on the variety and type of white wine being produced, a vintner must now decide whether or not to leave skins in contact with the juice. For lighter, aromatic wines, such as White Riesling, or for simple white table wines, skins are usually separated from the juice at this stage. This can be done simply by draining the juice from the tank or by running it over some type of screen device or press that separates juice from the skins.

For some varieties, such as Sauvignon Blanc or Chardonnay, a vintner may choose to leave the skins in contact with the juice for 2 to 24 hours in order to extract varietal flavor and aroma.

After the contact period, juice is drained from the tank and clarified by settling, filtration, or centrifuging. Meanwhile, the skins are pressed to extract all remaining juice. We refer to the first fraction as "free run" juice and the latter as "press" juice. The latter is generally fermented and aged separately. At some later stage, if the press fraction is of sufficient quality, it may be blended back with the free run. It can also be blended into an inferior wine or be distilled to brandy. In any case, at this point the yeast culture is added and fermentation is begun.

Fermentation temperatures in white wines can range from as low as 45° F to as high as 75° F. In a modern winery, wines are produced in stainless-steel tanks equipped with jackets through which propylene glycol is circulated. The fermentation process gives off heat, but a vintner can set the cooling control at a maximum temperature. If this temperature is exceeded, the cooling system automatically turns on. Lower temperatures slow the process and help maintain flavor and aroma components in the wine.

A vintner may need to use each tank three or more times during a season. The temperature must be set low enough to achieve a desired quality, yet high enough to finish the process within a reasonable time. Fermentation may take from three days to three weeks, depending on the sugar content of the grapes and the temperature of the "must." There are very special occasions when it can take longer than three weeks. Some varieties, such as Chardonnay, are fermented dry. The vintner lets the process run its course until all the natural grape-sugar has been converted into ethyl alcohol and carbon dioxide. In table wine production, carbon dioxide is allowed to escape.

For certain varieties, such as Chenin Blanc or White Riesling, some natural or residual sugar is desirable. Several methods are used in premium wine production to retain sugar. One technique involves fermenting most of a wine dry, while setting aside some unfermented grape juice to add back before bottling. The Germans refer to this unfermented grape juice as "sweet reserve." Alternatively, wine can be fermented down to the desired sugar level and then refrigerated and filtered to inhibit further action by the yeast.

A vintner must also decide whether to ferment wine in oak or stainless steel. Oak barrel fermentation imparts a distinctive character, so wines made this way are quite different from those that undergo the process in stainless steel, and are later aged in oak. Until recently, most California wines were made in stainless steel. Today more types of wine, such as Chardonnay, are produced in oak barrels. To me, this kind of decision is part of the art in winemaking. It is also the part I enjoy most. I might taste ten different Chardonnays and like them all for different reasons. Among those ten wines, some may be fermented in stainless and never see oak. Others might be fermented in stainless, and aged in oak, while a third group is fermented and aged in oak. All might be quite good. Your reaction to each is a matter of personal preference.

My own opinion is that oak aroma and flavor must be subtle, making a wine more complex and interesting. But when its character can be identified as oak, I consider it a defect. Of course, some wine drinkers might prefer oak aroma and flavor to that of Chardonnay. I'm sure they'll take exception to my preference.

A vintner monitors fermentation carefully. The wine is sampled at least once a day, usually more often. Temperature and sugar percentages are recorded. Because ethyl alcohol interferes greatly with the working of the refractometer, a hydrometer is used at this stage to measure the depletion of sugar by yeast. A hydrometer simply measures specific density, but accurate readings are difficult to obtain. The carbon dioxide produced during fermentation can buoy the hydrometer and cause a false reading. In addition, because alcohol is less dense than water, wine will not be dry—sugar free—until the hydrometer reads in a minus range, indicating that the new product is less dense than water, which is rated zero. The "dry" reading depends on how much alcohol is produced during fermentation. For a typical red table wine, it's about minus 1.5 degrees Brix at 12 to 13 percent alcohol.

When fermentation has run its course, or has been stopped short deliberately, a vintner usually filters or centrifuges the wine to remove solids and yeast remnants. Some wineries in France and a few in California leave the yeast remnants in the barrels and agitate the contents with a mixer or beater once or twice a day for several weeks. They feel that this imparts desirable characteristics to certain varieties of wine, such as Chardonnay or Sauvignon (Fumé) Blanc. This practice is referred to as "sur lees." It is not common in California.

At this stage, a vintner might adjust sulfur dioxide and total acidity levels to inhibit further microbial action. Although in winemaking, we use certain microbes, such as yeast and bacteria, to bring about desired effects, we must at the same time repress other microorganisms. In Chapter 8 we discussed, for example, why acetic acid bacteria, which converts ethyl alcohol to vinegar, is always undesirable and should be eliminated. We also looked at reasons why lactic acid bacteria, which converts malic to lactic acid, is desirable in some wines but not others.

But let's return to the question of oak-barrel versus stainless-steel. A fruity table wine, such as Johannisberg Riesling, may never touch oak. These wines usually go straight from stainless steel to the bottle. On the other hand, Chardonnay, or a similar wine, may be aged in oak tanks or barrels to add complexity.

Different types of oak have different effects on the aroma and flavor of a wine. American oak, Yugoslavian oak, and French oak are most commonly used in the wine business. Limousin and Never are the two most widely used types of French oak.

We must decide which combinations of wine and oak work best. This is again a subjective judgment. A vintner starts with a mental picture of the style wine he wishes to produce. He achieves this by bringing various factors together in a harmonious and attractive fashion. In this regard, a vintner is an artist. One can compare five producers making one variety of wine from grapes from the same vineyard to five qualified painters using the same oils and canvasses to interpret one scene. Each one's result will be original, otherwise the world would be quite boring.

Elsewhere, I have referred to "cooperage," meaning bulk wine containers; they can be made of stainless, oak, redwood or anything else. A vintner must decide whether to age the wine and, if so, how to age it. Wine can be aged in oak, redwood or stainless steel cooperage, as well as in bottles. When the wine has completed its aging period, whether for one week or one year, it is time to prepare for bottling.

Wine may or may not be blended at this stage. In general, blending means putting together wines from different containers. For instance, one may have various barrels or tanks of the same variety and simply want to make a large, uniform blend before bottling. He may add some portion of the pressed wine back to the free run, or he may blend two varieties of wine, such as Sauvignon Blanc and Semillon for complexity.

If a vintner blends, he cannot list the vintage year on the bottle unless 95 percent of the wine in it was made in the year designated. If he names the grape variety, 75 percent of the blend must be made from that variety. If he names a district, or appellation, 75 percent of the wine must be made from grapes grown there. Vineyard-designated wines—such as "Bonny's Vineyard"—must be 95 percent grapes from the named property.

The next stage is "finishing." We use various techniques to stabilize the wine and get it ready for bottling. For example, I may add egg whites or gelatin to extract astringent substances. I may also use Bentonite, a special clay, to remove protein. Potassium acid tartrate (cream of tartar) can be precipitated from wine chilled to 28° F for 3 to 14 days

A vintner's aim is to prevent cloudiness or sediment which might make the bottled wine unmarketable. Under warm conditions, proteins will cause a haze, particularly in white wines. These wines might not always be stored properly, in a warehouse, a store, or a home. It is, therefore, desirable to treat them with Bentonite to make them heat-stable. Bentonite has an electrical charge opposite to proteins and thus the two will precipitate out.

If wine is exposed to cold conditions, either during shipment or in a home refrigerator, potassium and tartaric acid can form cream of tartar on the cork or in the bottom of the bottle. Cream of tartar is a natural ingredient of wine; it does not cause undesirable flavors or aromas. Many knowledgeable wine drinkers consider the presence of tartrates to be a sign that a vintage has not been overprocessed. These savants simply decant the wine off the sediment before serving it. But lower-priced wines are usually cold-stabilized to prevent tartrates in the bottle, since cream of tartar might be considered a defect by the less knowledgeable.

In my opinion, sediment in a bottle of wine is neither a plus or minus factor in quality. The question is whether or not any undesirable aromas or flavors might be associated with the sediment. In most cases, sediment has no effect on quality, but it is never pleasant to drink the last glass from a bottle of wine and end up with a half teaspoon of cream of tartar in your mouth. That's why we usually remove tartrates.

Once the wine has been stabilized, it is generally filtered to assure that it will be clear. Cellulose pads, diatomaceous earth, and membrane filters are used for this purpose. In many wineries sterile filters with pore sizes as small as .45 microns are used, especially in dealing with products with residual sugar. The pore size of a sterile filter is small enough that yeast, and even bacteria, cannot pass. By removing these microbes, we make sure that no fermentation takes place in the bottle. It is also possible to pasteurize the wine by warming it to 180° F or by using a preservative such as sorbic acid to kill the microbes. But for premium-quality wine, sterile filtration is considered better by far.

After a wine is bottled, it may or may not be "bottle aged." Light, fruity wines are frequently shipped directly to market. A period of six months to a year in the bottle may enhance the character of a nice Chardonnay.

RED WINE

The best glass of white wine is the first,
the best glass of red wine is the last.
ANONYMOUS

Red wine production varies significantly from the process we've just described. Red grapes are crushed and stemmed shortly after harvest. Most vintners remove all the stems before fermentation. A few favor putting some stems back during the fermentation of certain varieties, particularly Pinot Noir. I'm not an advocate of this, but then I hope never to produce another Pinot Noir in my lifetime.

Theoretically, you can make a white wine from red grapes by removing the skins from the juice immediately after crushing. Thus, for years now, in Europe and the United States, Pinot Noir has been used as one of the base grapes for champagne or sparkling wine production. Moreover, we are seeing today the popularity of Blanc de Noir or "blush" wines. Literally, this means white from dark, which alludes to the fact that we are making white wines from varieties which are traditionally considered red. White Zinfandel is the most popular example.

After destemming and beginning fermentation, a yeast culture is added. Typical red wine fermentation temperatures might be 70° to 85° F. Grape skins have a tendency to float to the top because of the buoyancy effect of carbon dioxide produced, and they form a "cap." This simply refers to the mass of skins which rise to the top of fermenting juice. To extract the color from skins, the cap must be punched down or moistened regularly. It is also necessary to keep the cap moist to prevent the formation of acetic acid. One approach to doing this involves pumping juice from the bottom of a tank and circulating it back over the skins. A more modern method is to use a rotary fermentation tank, a device that somewhat resembles a cement mixer.

Depending on what style of wine a vintner wishes to make, the "cap" may be removed earlier or later in the fermentation process. A light red wine with little tannin (substances that cause puckeriness in a red wine) and color requires less skin contact time than a full-bodied, dark red wine. Typically, a winery might pump juice over the cap twice a day for 20 minutes until fermentation reaches 5° to 0° Brix before drawing off the free-run juice and pressing the cap. As with white wines, the pressed fraction is kept separate from the free run.

Usually the amount of color desired determines when you separate a fermenting wine from skins. Studies indicate that, after a certain time, no more color is extracted from skins, but additional tannins are drawn out. While tannins play an important role in the aging of a red wine, they can be over emphasized.

Other studies have shown that, while tannins continue to be extracted, after a certain point they begin to lose their puckeriness. Some vintners leave skins on the wine for a week or two after it has fermented dry. They believe that this practice extracts more desirable elements and softens the tannins. This method is referred to as prolonged or extended maceration.

Premium reds are often inoculated with lactic acid bacteria at the same time as or shortly after the yeast strain is added. The resulting malolactic fermentation produces a certain complexity of aroma. Also, it helps make a softer, less sour wine.

After 5 to 10 days, juice is usually fermented dry of residual sugar and malic acid. Even if two wines have no residual sugar, I often hear people say that one is dryer than the other. I think they're referring to the fact that one has higher acidity or a more tart taste than the other. Sometimes, too, wines with higher alcohol levels have greater glycerol content, which gives the wine a fuller, smoother, almost sweet taste.

When the sugar is converted, we may add sulfur dioxide to prevent further microbial action. Total acidity may also be adjusted if it is felt this is necessary for taste and balance. It's permissible by California law to use tartaric, citric, or some other acid for this purpose. Proper acid level means that a wine is neither too tart nor too flat. Generally, tartness is not a problem in California. Because of our climate, we usually grow grapes with good sugar content but slightly low acid.

Flat wines, however, can be a problem. If you've ever left a soft drink or beer out overnight and tasted it the next day, you know what I mean by "flat." Carbon dioxide in solution will produce carbonic acid. The escape of the carbon dioxide and the loss of carbonic acid from an open soft drink or beer causes that "flat" taste. A producer's goal, by adjusting acidity, is to produce a wine with proper acid balance.

Wine improves with age; the older
I get, the better I like it.
ANONYMOUS

It is common for premium red wines to be aged in oak barrels. During that aging process, wine will clarify, oxidize, and extract some aroma and flavor components from the wood. Clarification occurs by settling, filtering, or centrifuging before barrel aging. If it is not clarified before putting it into barrels, pumping and labor costs will be very high in order to assure that the sediment does not decompose, causing undesirable odors in the finished product.

Some oxidation is necessary during aging. Oxygen reacts chemically with substances known as polyphenols. Color pigments and tannins are both polyphenols. As oxygen reacts with a red wine, the color changes from purple in its youth, to red, and eventually tawny, in its old age. Thus, color is a good indication of a wine's age.

As oxygen reacts with tannins, longer chemical chains are formed. An aged red will then be less puckery or astringent. This is why older reds, which have had more time to form these longer tannin chains, tend to be softer and more pleasant to the taste. In older wines these longer chain tannins may precipitate out of solution, causing a slight sediment not harmful to the quality of the wine.

It was once thought that wines age because they "breathe" through oak barrels and, after being bottled, through corks. This is not true. Many of us put our Cabernet Sauvignon in the barrels, roll them slightly so that the bung, or stopper, is at a 2 o'clock position. It now forms a tighter seal with the barrel because it is always in contact with the wine. Within a few days or weeks, a vacuum develops in the barrel. Because of this vacuum, we can leave the wine an entire year without topping it and still form no acetic acid or vinegar, even though there might be three-percent head-space within the barrel after a year's time.

If a barrel leaks or some wine evaporates over a period of time, conversion to vinegar might be expected. This would happen if there were oxygen in the head-space because acetic acid bacteria requires oxygen to function. But if a barrel is rolled to 2 o'clock, even if head-space develops within it, no acetic acid is formed. If the container breathed, as was formerly thought, head space would contain oxygen and vinegar would be produced. Formation of a vacuum in a well-sealed barrel is proof positive that properly sealed containers do not breathe. Periodic opening of the barrels, or pumping of the wine, will provide all the oxygen necessary for proper aging.

Once the vintner has determined that a red has had sufficient barrel aging, it is time to prepare for bottling. As with whites, the vintner may or may not choose to blend. He will also finish the wine, although reds generally do not require as much attention at this stage. Protein is not usually a problem in a red wine, since it and tannins are oppositely charged and generally do not exist together. As a result, the use of Bentonite with reds is not as common as with whites. A vintner may choose to use egg whites or gelatin to remove tannins and thus further soften a blend before bottling. Because most premium red wines will not be refrigerated before serving, a vintner may also choose not to cold-stabilize. My own feeling is that I'd rather have a slight amount of sediment than overwork a wine to the extent that I remove its character.

ROSÉ WINE

Finally, let me offer a word about Rosé wines. Some Rosé wines are produced simply by blending approximately two-thirds or more white with a red. For better quality Rosés, a vintner might start with a Zinfandel, a Gamay, or a Grenache, and limit skin contact time to 6 or 8 hours. This will give him all the color he needs for a nice blush.

If you are a home winemaker, I offer three observations: One of the most common problems with homemade wine is that fermentation slows down at the end, either because of lack of nutrients for the yeast or because the cellar temperature is cold enough to impede or stop the process. If wine is bottled over the winter under cold conditions, come spring and summer, warmer temperatures might cause fermentation to begin again in the bottle. Many home winemakers have told me about waking up at night to the sound of bottles exploding in the cellar. There is no real reason, to my knowledge, that they should blow up at night rather than in daytime. Most likely, the home winemaker was working during the day and didn't hear them exploding then.

Another nemesis of home winemakers is reused barrels which have not been sterilized properly. They contain acetic acid bacteria which quickly turns their wine to vinegar.

My final observation is that homemade wines are the curse of a professional vintner's life. Frequently when it comes up in a conversation that I own a winery, someone says, "Oh, I make wine at home. Let me get you a bottle so you can try it." After tasting it, I generally form the opinion that the person would do better to give up and buy a nice cheap jug wine at his favorite store. Frequently, homemade wines almost take the enamel off your teeth. Then the producer proudly comments, "You can't make wines like that." Thanks to U.C. Davis, I hope he's right.

"Here's to champagne, the drink divine,
that makes us forget our troubles;
it's made of a dollar's worth of wine
and three dollars worth of bubbles."

ANONYMOUS

10.
Other Grape Products

This book has been devoted primarily to table wines, to their production and use, but I'd like to take some time to discuss other "grape products," namely sparkling wine or champagne, dessert and appetizer wines, and brandy.

We can start with a wine classification chart taken from *Wine, An Introduction,* by Maynard Amerine and Vernon Singleton. It doesn't represent all types of wine produced in the world but it does include the more important ones and the types you're likely to be acquainted with. The chart will give you an idea of how each fits into the overall pattern of production.

A. *"Natural" wines,* 9 to 14 percent alcohol (nature and keeping qualities depend heavily on protection from air and on a "complete" yeast fermentation).
    I. *Still wines* (no evident carbon dioxide)
        a. Dry (no noticeable sweetness) table wines, intended for use during meals
           1. White

    2. Rosé (pink)

    3. Red

    (Further subclasses are based primarily on grape variety or on region of origin)

  b. Slightly sweet table wines ("mellow," "vino" types)

    1. White

    2. Rosé (pink)

    3. Red

  c. Sweet table wines

    1. White

    2. Rosé (pink)

  d. Specialty wines

    1. Slightly carbonated types: red, rosé (pink), and white

    2. Flavored table wines: red, rosé (pink), and white

 II. *Sparkling wines* (appreciable carbon dioxide under pressure)

  a. White (champagne, sparkling muscat)

  b. Rosé (pink champagne)

  c. Red (sparkling burgundy, cold duck)

B. *Dessert and appetizer wines,* "generous" wines, 15 to 21 percent alcohol (nature and "keeping" qualities depend heavily on the addition of wine spirits)

 I. Sweet wines

  a. White (muscatel, white port, angelica)

  b. Pink (California tokay, tawny port)

  c. Red (port, black muscat)

 II. *Sherries* (white sweet or dry wines with oxidized flavors)

  a. Aged types

  b. Flor sherry types (secondary aerobic yeast fermentation)

  c. Baked types

III. *Flavored,* specialty wines (usually white port base)

  a. Vermouth (pale dry, French; sweet types, Italian)

  b. Proprietary products

    1. Special natural wines

    2. Other "brand name" specialty wines

SPARKLING WINE

Sparkling wines or champagne, classified as those with excess carbon dioxide, deserve a more detailed discussion. Whether a producer calls them sparkling wines or champagne, they are still basically the same: a product with excess gas produced by a second fermentation. The French maintain that American producers do not have the right to use the words Champagne, Burgundy, Chablis, and Sauterne, because these are the names of specific areas in their country. I also hear this argument from the purists among American wine drinkers who explain to me that American producers should not use these terms. At the same time, these same critics enjoy Americanmade Swiss cheese, French bread, Italian ice cream, and numerous other products without becoming entangled in controversy. Because of my obvious disdain for such discriminations, I'll use the terms sparkling wine and champagne interchangeably.

Remember the discussion of fermentation in Chapter 8? Basically, in order to produce a sparkling wine, you simply take a finished product and cause a second yeast fermentation of sugar, this time trapping the carbon dioxide gas produced by the fermentation.

Earlier in this book, I referred to champagne as the probable result of a historical accident. Dom Perignon (1638-1715), a Benedictine monk of the Abbey of Hautvilliers in France, had fermented some white wine. Because of the cool cellar conditions, the fermentation became so slow that it appeared to have stopped. So he bottled the white wine. Obviously it still retained some residual sugar and yeast cells, because when cellar temperature warmed up again come spring, the wine fermented completely to dryness. Upon opening the wine, Dom Perignon found the "sparkle" to be enjoyable and unique. The discovery and production of sparkling wine would not have been possible, however, until the usefulness of cork was realized. This happened, supposedly, when other monks traveling from Spain stopped at the Abbey of Dom Perignon with their water flasks stoppered with cork.

The refinement of champagne production has made it a process separate and unique from table wine production, beginning with the choosing of grape varieties best suited for sparkling wine to the maturity at harvest. Generally, varietal character is not considered desirable—let alone of prime importance—in sparkling wines. Commonly, several kinds of grapes are blended: Chardonnay, Pinot Blanc, and Pinot Noir being among the most popular, so that in the end, subtlety rather than overpowering varietal character is the goal.

The grapes are harvested at lesser sugar content than for the typical table wine. The reasons are twofold: the first is that lower alcohol is desirable in the base wine (also called "cuvée"), since a second fermentation will produce additional alcohol. The second reason is that by harvesting at lower sugar, you will tend to have higher total acidity and lower pH, both of which are desirable for the crispness and longevity of a sparkling wine. During the primary fermentation, a cuvée may be treated like any other white wine, finished before the following spring in the manner described in Chapter 9, so it becomes protein-and-tartrate-stable and is filtered clear. Then a champagne producer puts together the tirage, which is a blend of base wine, yeast nutrient, and a source of sugar. In California this is one time during wine production when it is legal to use other than natural grape sugar—such as cane sugar (liquid or dry), corn syrup, honey or rock candy—in the process. It must be added back to the dry wine in order to provide a food source for yeast cells that will provide a second fermentation. This will again produce ethyl alcohol and carbon dioxide. Generally, the amount of sugar added is calculated to produce six atmospheres of carbon dioxide measured at 60° F. One atmosphere of gas is 15 lbs. per square inch, so the pressure in a bottle of sparkling wine can reach 90 lbs. per square inch. Thus, the need for heavy glass bottles, wire hoods to hold corks, and serious caution in opening a bottle of champagne.

There are two common methods for the production of sparkling wine. The traditional method is fermenting in the bottle *(methode champenoise)*. It is considered, by many, to produce superior quality. True or not, it certainly has more prestige. We will discuss it first.

Up to the point of putting together the tirage, the production of bottle-fermented or of bulk *(charmat)* processing are the same. If a cuvée is to be bottle-fermented, it is at this juncture that it is placed in a champagne bottle. A crown cap, the type of closure you see on a soft drink, is applied and bottles are laid down in a cellar to allow fermentation to take place within the bottle. Stainless steel crown caps are currently used because they will not rust in a cool, humid cellar. Depending upon the temperature of a cellar, fermentation will probably not take more than two weeks. But for bottle-fermented champagne to be truly different from that made by the bulk *(charmat)* process, sparkling wine must stay in contact with yeast cells for a longer period, from six months to two years, depending on the producer. During this time there is a breakdown of the yeast cells called "autolysis" in the bottle, which imparts to sparkling wine a desirable "yeasty" aroma and flavor. If desirable autolysis is not obvious in a wine, or if you do not appreciate it, you'd probably be better off buying a *charmat*-fermented sparkling wine at a substantially lower price.

At some stage when a champagne producer determines that there has been sufficient time on the yeast, he begins to remove sediment from the bottle, being careful not to lose any substantial amount of sparkle. The first step is called "riddling"; yeast and sediment are shaken down into the neck of an inverted bottle. Traditionally, this has been done in an A-frame rack called a riddling rack, which has holes into which the necks of the bottles are fitted. A mark is painted

RIDDLING RACK

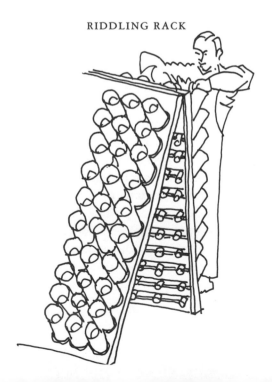

onto the bottom of each so that the riddler has a guage for how much he has turned a bottle each day. He will face the riddling rack with the push-up bottoms of the bottles protruding with a painted mark. Each day he will give each bottle a slight swirl, turn, and drop it back into the rack, daily increasing the upward angle of the bottom of each so that the sediment will collect in the neck against the crown cap, which is now inverted. Nowadays, during bottling, a small plastic cup (the "Bidule") is frequently inserted under the crown cap so that when the bottle ends up in its inverted position, sediment will collect in the cup. Some sparkling-wine producers are also using automatic riddling racks in which bottles are inverted and the entire rack (controlled by a timer) shakes one or more times a day. Another method is to place the bottles neck down in a bin. Each day a machine shakes the entire bin, again increasing its angle until the neck of a bottle is straight down and all sediment has been collected in the area of the crown cap.

The next step is "disgorging." A bottle, still in its inverted position, goes through a brine solution to refrigerate its neck to 5°F. This will freeze the sediment in it; a trained person can then turn the bottle at a more upright angle and take off the crown cap with a bottle opener, at which time the pressure will blow the plug of sediment out. Because carbon dioxide is far more soluble in liquid at lower temperatures, 5°F is calculated to freeze the sediment and cool the sparkling wine enough so that although the plug will be blown out, excessive sparkle will not be lost. After disgorging, sparkling wine should still have 5 to 5½ atmospheres of pressure.

The "dosage" is then added to the bottle. This is the term used to describe the possible blend of wine, sweetener and even brandy, which is added to refill the bottle after the loss by disgorging. The formula for dosage will vary, as determined both by a producer and by the amount of sweetness wanted in the final product. For all producers you can expect the "brut" to be the driest. Foreigners use terms such as sec, demi-sec, and doux, to denote increasing degrees of sweetness in a particular bottling. The demi-sec and doux are definitely considered dessert-type sparkling wines. Amazingly enough, however, in American parlance "extra dry" is sweeter than brut.

A less labor-intensive method of producing sparkling wine is the

124

charmat or bulk process. As I mentioned, up to the time of putting together the tirage, bulk and bottle-fermented processes are identical. You should be aware that since the charmat champagnes tend to be lower priced, producers may also use some lesser-priced varieties of grapes, such as French Colombard, Chenin Blanc, or even Thompson Seedless. However, that is not to say that the better charmat sparkling wines might not use the other "champagne" varieties. German sparkling wines (Sekt) are made from Riesling and other hybrid varieties.

For the charmat process, the tirage, is fermented in a larger tank in which the carbon dioxide is trapped. You might picture this vessel as a rather large bottle. Quality control in the Charmat process is better than that in bottle fermentation since the temperature can be better controlled. Temperature control is important because a lower reading causes a slower fermentation, producing smaller bubbles in the champagne. Smaller bubbles produce effervescence in the glass for a longer period of time. I must openly confess, however, that I cannot tell a small champagne bubble from a large one!

After the two weeks of fermentation and two weeks of refrigeration at approximately 22°F to settle out yeast, the sparkling wine is filtered and bottled at the same low temperature. This temperature, plus counter-pressure with nitrogen, will maintain carbon dioxide in solution until a cork and wire hood are applied. The biggest problem might be to adhere labels on a "sweating" bottle. This is accomplished by passing the bottled product through a warm water bath or through an infrared tunnel to heat the bottles to just above dew point. The labels are then applied with ice-proof glue.

Pink sparkling wines, red sparkling wines, or sparkling Muscats, are produced by using one of the above described processes, but they start with different base wines. Cold Duck, which was the rage a few years ago, has nothing to do with shivering fowl. The name comes from a German pun based on the words "kalte ende" ("cold end," or "leftover") and "kalte ente ("cold duck"). Servants of German party-goers poured together the leftover red and white wines and humorously called them cold duck. The term cold duck describes a sparkling wine made up of half sparkling burgundy and half champagne. It probably doesn't matter at this stage, since today we could probably describe that rage as "dead duck."

DESSERT WINES

Basically, these are wines in the 17 to 20 percent alcohol range; the sweetness level of the final product determines whether they are appetizer or dessert wines.

The most popular white dessert wines are the muscat class. Today we don't see much white port or angelica. Sweet or cream sherry will be discussed in a moment. To make the general styles of white dessert wine, you must first separate juice from skins. Fermentation is started, since by law juice must ferment one degree sugar before brandy is added. The purpose of adding brandy is to obtain alcohol without having to ferment the natural sugar, which remains to give the wine its dessert character. The stage of fermentation at which brandy is added will determine the sugar content of the resulting wine. When brandy is added to produce 17 to 20 percent alcohol, it will stop the fermentation because the yeast can no longer function at this alcohol-level. Since alcohol is less dense than water at zero, you must remember that the addition of alcohol will reduce sugar level both by dilution and by adding alcohol with a lower specific gravity. All this must be calculated by a vintner. Bentonite is then added to make the wine protein stable before filtering. The product is then put into barrels for aging and if a total acid or sulfur dioxide adjustment is required, it can be done at this time.

Red dessert wines are made in a similar fashion but the vintner does not wish to add brandy while juice is in contact with skins, because too much brandy will be lost in pressing. He extracts the red color by heating the "must" to somewhere between 140° and 180° F, circulating wine back over the "cap" until sufficient color is extracted. This might be a two to eight hour process. He then draws off the red juice and adds yeast to begin fermentation and, as he does with the white dessert wine, determines at which point of fermentation to add 190+ proof grape brandy.

Common red dessert wines are made from varieties such as Carignane, Petite Sirah, Salvador, Alicante Bouschet, Ruby Red, and Royalty. More traditional and varietal ports can be made from Tinta

Madeira, Touriga, Souzao, and Zinfandel. Recently I have tasted some very fine Zinfandel and Cabernet Sauvignon Ports. Red dessert wines are clarified, filtered, and aged in a manner similar to the one described for white dessert wines.

SHERRY

A special category of wine in this 17 to 20 percent alcohol range is sherry. It is a traditional wine in which some of the ethanol has been oxidized to acetaldehyde, which gives the wine its peculiar aroma and flavor. As I said at the beginning, it is common folklore that this was probably an accident and we could consider sherry to be simply a badly oxidized white wine. Because people grew used to this style and began to like it, vintners now take perfectly good wines and convert them to sherry. There are three ways this can happen. The first is simply to let a wine age until it overoxidizes and takes on the sherry or acetaldehyde character. In commercial production two other methods are used: (1) baking and (2) using a special yeast strain.

For a baked sherry, vintners start with a sherry material, a base wine to which 190+ proof brandy has been added, bringing it to 17-19 percent alcohol. Natural grape-sweetening material (concentrate) can be added if the sherry is to be something other than dry. It is then warmed to between 120° and 140°F for a period of 45 to 128 days. When he determines that he has achieved the degree of baked-sherry character he desires, he will age, finish, and bottle the wine, using methods described previously. Baked sherry is sometimes described as having a "nutty" flavor and aroma.

The other method involves the use of a yeast. This used to be referred to as "flor" sherry because the flor yeast would float on the surface of the wine and as the yeast cells propogated and multiplied, they did so in a pattern that resembled a flower. A more modern method is called the submerged culture sherry yeast; it does not float on the surface, but when mixed in the sherry material with oxygen, it will produce similar flavor and aroma components as found in flor sherry. Sherry material is generally 14 to 15½ percent alcohol when yeast is added. When yeast has produced the amount of aldehydes which a vintner wishes (approximately 800-900 parts per million), alcohol can then be adjusted up to 17 or 18 percent by the addition of brandy; then the wine is filtered and aged, later to be finished and bottled.

If you are fond of sherry, you may have run across the term "solera." This term is sometimes used in connection with other dessert wines also. It describes a method of only removing half the aged wine from a barrel and replacing it with a wine one year younger. If this is done year after year, at some point the solera system will begin to consistently produce a wine of an average age based on the number of tiers in the solera. Solera systems are used to produce consistency of quality and of age.

BRANDY

The final grape product that I'll include in this discussion is brandy. Around the world brandy has many aliases. It is called Cognac, Armagnac, "Eau de Vie" (meaning "water of life"), Grappa—and I'm sure you might think of a few more. The process by which each of these is made might be slightly different, but basically brandy is the product of grape-wine distillation. Distillation is the separation of components of a mixture as determined by the boiling point of each. Therefore, it is a given that you must start with wine before you can produce brandy.

It is easy enough to understand how early man might have made the first wine accidentally, but this is not true of brandy. Distillation is not a natural process in the sense that if left alone, wine will not convert to brandy. The inventor of distillation would have had to understand two important facts. One, it is necessary to have an alcoholic product, i.e., wine, in order to begin. (When I was about 13 an older cousin came home from chemistry class and announced that we would make apricot brandy. We stripped the tree and boiled the apricots to death only to make apricot butter. Evidently he had slept through the part of the lecture that you had to ferment the apricots first.) Two, the alcohol can be vaporized by heating the wine and then recondensing. This would separate alcohol from other components of wine, principally water, and thus concentrate alcohol into a higher proof product. As a general rule, you concentrate a product by heating it to 212° F, to boil off water and leave the higher boiling point ingredients. But since ethyl alcohol is an ingredient that vaporizes at 173° F, it will be driven off and collected long before the water in wine comes to boil. Even if the inventor of distillation had realized that he could obtain higher proof alcohol by concentration, I wonder how he discovered that when he heated wine, he would have to trap and recondense ethyl alcohol before his product reached its visible boiling point. If you study the history of distillation, you will find that its discovery is not attributed to any one person. It was probably a long evolutionary process. One source believes that the first real distiller was probably a first or second century Greek-Egyptian alchemist, who, in an attempt to transmute base metal into gold, boiled some wine in a crude still.

There are two modern methods for making brandy. One is the pot-still or batch method; the other is the continuous or column still. In both methods, wine is heated until its alcohol vaporizes. Alcohol vapors then pass through cooling coils where they are recondensed to liquid and collected. Whiskey, bourbon, and scotch are made in a similar manner, the principal difference being that they are grain products that, before distillation, must first be malted and fermented to produce beer. Whiskey, bourbon and scotch are, therefore, beer distillates.

The illustration is a diagram of a continuous or column still. The stripping column on the right is where wine and steam are introduced. Because the top of the stripping column is less than 212° F, water remains in that column, whereas alcohol vapors go to a rectifying column. Within alcohol vapors are the higher alcohols, such as acetaldehyde, sometimes referred to as "heads," which have a boiling point of approximately 70° F. They will go to the top of a rectifying column seeking the coolest area. Ethyl alcohol or product will recondense at approximately 173° F at 160 to 170 proof. The lower alcohols or fusel oils will recondense at 183° F or 135 proof. Remember that "proof" is twice alcohol percentage; therefore, 100 proof alcohol is 50 percent alcohol.

With a column-still, a distiller is able to make a fine separation between the fusel oils, the ethyl alcohol, and higher alcohols thus obtaining what I would describe as a "cleaner" and less-hot product. A

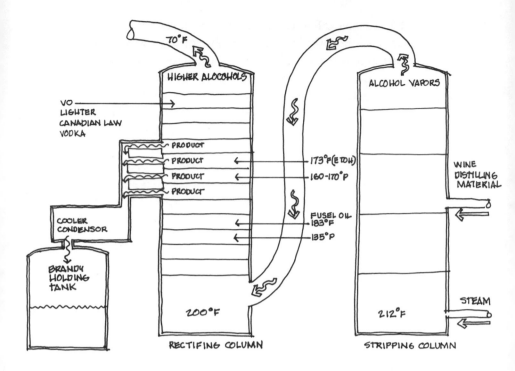

BRANDY-MAKING PROCESS

cognac-type brandy is produced by the use of a pot still in which the wine is heated and, for a calculated amount of time, higher alcohols which vaporize at a lower temperature are allowed to escape. At some point a distiller begins to collect a product within which he will have the last of the higher alcohols, all or most of the ethanol, and some of the lower alcohols before he stops collecting. Because he cannot separate higher and lower alcohols from ethyl alcohol, as in the continuous still, he tends to obtain a heavier, hotter product. Of course, this is all a matter of taste and if you like cognac, you might find California brandy too neutral. Since I got my start in winemaking with Christian Brothers, and like their lighter style of brandy, I find cognac much too heavy for my palate.

The prices of these various wine products are affected substantially by tax rates. Table wine is taxed at 17 cents a gallon, Federal Excise Tax; whereas, dessert wines with 17 percent alcohol and more, jump up to 64 cents a gallon. Sparkling wine is $3.40 a gallon, and brandy, which used to be $10.50, climbed in October of 1985 to $12.50 per gallon, matching the cost on other spirits. As in most things we do in life, we're working (and drinking) about half the time for the government. Luckily, I prefer a good dry white or red table wine to champagne. But if you prefer sparkling wine, even granting that additional labor and other costs are involved, the tax rate shouldn't jump 20 times—from 17 cents to $3.40 a gallon! Uncle Sam is simply assessing a luxury tax on you every time you enjoy a glass of champagne. Years ago the German government discovered that if it lowered the tax of its sparkling wine from $3.40 to $1.00 a gallon, people drank a lot more sparkling wine so that the government actually collected more revenue in the long run. I don't see that happening here because so many people in our society and government have a prohibitionist mentality. The government has become too dependent on the "sin" tax on wine and champagne to support their spending habits.

Wine is, indeed, a living thing,
brash in its youth, full-
blossoming in its maturity, but
subject, if not used in time, to
senility, decay, and death.

ANDRÉ L. SIMON

II.

Reflections in a Wine Glass

It's said that "work is the curse of the drinking class." My father drank and labored. Lord knows I drink my share, so I'll most likely toil the rest of my life. But if you have to bear that heavy yoke (work), being a winegrower is a nice way to go. There's an added dimension compared to most businesses.

That's not always good. How many other businessmen's friends request a visit to the jobsite on weekends? You see, wine's a hobby to these folks—something they do in their spare time. They want to talk about it, learn more, sample more. Generally I share their enthusiasm. There are occasions when I must say "no," because it's time to be with the family. Our winery is closed on Sundays by design. And our hospitality staff knows better than to call me at home on Saturdays.

But when people are genuinely interested in wine and don't impose themselves on my private time, I love to visit and sample.

I don't feel like a public figure and will never get used to autographing things. Yet I always oblige when asked. I do feel honored to see my product in fine wine shops and restaurants as I travel the country. To walk into a restaurant for the first time, incognito, and upon ordering your own wine, have the waiter tell you that it's the best on the list, always evokes a big tip, and an extra bottle for the staff to share after work.

There are times when you get preferential treatment because you are known—like a reservation when the restaurant would be "full" to someone else. That's nice. There are other times when the waiter or someone else wants to talk wine when you just want to eat dinner or visit with your wife.

Vintners don't get rich. They opt for a pleasant lifestyle and, if successful, lead a financially comfortable life. In short, they are glorified farmers. They just happen to process a farm product to which a certain amount of mystique is attached. Yet, for their income level, vintners probably travel more of the country, stay at nicer hotels and eat in more good restaurants than most people. Yet this is to promote the product. I would rather stay home and tend the barrels. But when I do travel, it is not uncommon to run across a neighboring vintner in an airport or far off city. Statistics indicate that we are not doing a very good job of increasing the number of aficionados of wine so we compete for the attention and patronage of the same limited audience. Thus, at any given time, there may be as many vintners on the promotion trail as at the winery.

And if successful, he'll probably be land rich and cash poor, building a nice estate for his children and the IRS. If not successful in this very capital intensive business, he may even go belly up. As one old joke says it, "the way to make a small fortune in the wine business is to start with a large fortune."

So why would anyone want to be a vintner? Why do I enjoy it so much? First of all, I like to think there is a certain artistic ability to being a winegrower. I take pride in what I do and I derive great satisfaction when other people enjoy it. I have always had the vision that wine is food and have always expected my food to taste good, to be enjoyable, so I have produced wines designed to evoke the same response.

I remember when I started my own winery in the early 70s with this concept of wine as food. I always tried to produce an elegant wine, typified by finesse rather than power. When I started the winery, I decided to make only Cabernet Sauvignon which would not be released until the fifth year. So there I was with years of inventory of these elegant, finesse-styled wines building up, while at the same time many wine producers and most wine writers were into "big, monster, tannic, red wines," the kind that will take the enamel off your teeth. It was very stylish to equate tannin and unapproachability with future quality. You'd think from their comments that good-tasting wines had no potential whatsoever. It was a little unnerving because if that tendency was more than a fad, I was in big trouble.

It has been somewhat reassuring to me to see that most of those "monster" types are no longer with us. I think I can safely say that most producers today are swinging back toward more elegant, "food styled" wines. Unfortunately, the term "food wine" is taking a rap because some producers have decided to make lighter styles and call them "food wines," not having taken the time or made the investment to produce a wine with much character, then age it enough to produce an elegant, fine style. Today, even in Burgundy and Bordeaux, France, we see the same kind of argument raging. Some European producers claim they must get back to the bigger versions which established their reputation. Granted these wines take many years to reach their peak.

The entire controversy over whether to produce a lighter wine which can be drunk sooner or to produce a more full-bodied, heavier edition is dictated by consumers—what they will buy and how long they are willing to age it. People like to talk about older wines but few have the cellar, the patience or the capital to age reds to any reasonable degree; therefore, our industry has taken the approach that if this is what the consumer wants and is willing to pay for, this is what we will offer them.

Some of us who are willing to take the financial risk hold our wines longer. We do this because we see wine making as an art form and because we realize that a good red wine takes time to come around. All this must be calculated into your business plan and that's why this industry is so capital intensive. It takes three years to harvest any fruit from a newly planted vineyard. Then, in the sixth through eighth years, the vineyard may reach full production. It then produces a full crop for the next 30 to 40 years before it begins to decline. During those first six to eight years of the vineyard's life, while it is producing less than a full crop, you can expect cash deficits to pile up. Then, at least if you're only growing the grapes to sell, you begin to enjoy some income. But if you choose to be a winegrower, you're not only faced with no grape sales and the additional capital investment of a winery, but one to three more years aging for a premium white and three to five years minimum for a premium red, which could add up to ten years of deficits. You have to really love the wine business and be a little crazy to stay in it.

Let's address some common recurring questions in this business such as, "When will this wine be at its peak?" My answer is, "When you think it's wonderful." I'd venture to say that only about 5 percent of wine drinkers have a wine cellar of any reasonable size where they can hope to buy and hold reds until they reach maturity. I believe that statistics indicate that approximately 30 percent of Americans drink wine on a regular basis. If 5 percent of that number store wine, we're saying about only 1 to 2 percent of the population has a reasonably sized cellar. All of this being said, most American consumers drink it, if not the same night they bought a bottle, then within 6 months to a year of that time. Any intelligent wine producer should take this into consideration in his marketing plan and in determining the style of his product.

There may be subtle but important differences between light, soft and elegant products. These differences might be determined by the supply of grapes, fermentation techniques, blending varieties, or the amount of time given to age the product before it goes to market. Frequently I'm asked what other grape varieties do I blend with Cabernet Sauvignon, the insinuation being that if the wine is 100 percent Cabernet, it might be less complex. I like to counter the suggestion by saying that since I give my wines considerably longer aging in both barrel and bottle, I don't need to use varieties with lighter tannin in order to ready them more quickly for the market-place. But the reality is that if one artisan thinks he can make a finer product by using 100 percent varietal, while the other chooses to blend, I think they should have the freedom to do so. Vintners have a way of doing things pragmatically, then backing into their marketing plan to justify what they did in the first place.

An argument can also be developed to counter those who would claim that you can only make a fine red wine by using French Never oak for aging. You'll find that if you visited five wineries, you'd get five different versions of how to do the job properly. You see, vintners, like most artists, have strong egos, and my own attitude is if it works for them, bless them; just don't let them claim it's the only way.

Because wine is my passion, I stock a large personal cellar. It covers about 800 sq. ft. and holds 5,000 bottles. I arrived at the size rather simply. My wife wanted a good-sized pool in which to swim laps. I figured if she could have a 700- to 800-square-foot pool, I could have a wine cellar the same size. I also began to collect vintages for each of my children with the hope that when they were 21 years old, I could present them each with a 2,400-bottle cellar going back to their birth years. (When I've told this story to wine groups, I've had many solicitations for adoption.) The kids now average about halfway to the drinking age and, unfortunately, their wine is taking up too much space in my cellar. The problem may cure itself because as I run out of some of the vintages from my own collection. I may start dipping into theirs—just to make sure everything's aging properly, of course!

Having a cellar this size permits me the luxury of drinking older wines and I don't drink just wines I've produced. Whenever I taste something I like—and you must remember that my cellar contains probably 90 percent reds—I'll buy seven cases, one for each of the kids and four for me. My bins hold four cases each and I figure if I'm paying the tab, I get the lion's share. In this way I can drink five- to ten-year-old wines on a regular basis to determine how I think they're aging and if they've reached their peak. Once it occurs to me that a wine has peaked (again, let me emphasize that this is a subjective judgment), I tend to drink up the balance of the inventory a little quicker.

Once I tasted wines with one of my professors whom I respected very much. Most of the samples were a similar age but I threw in one much older that I thought was "pruney" and "over the hill." It turned out to be his favorite. As I reflected on it, I came to the conclusion that all his life he had been able to drink older wines than I; therefore, he had come to appreciate what a good old wine tasted like. I believe that most consumers today are used to drinking tannic two- to three-year-old reds and it will be a while before we educate them to appreciate well-aged reds.

Another common question is, "How long will this wine age?" That's simple—until "it's over the hill." The quote at the head of the chapter said it very well: A wine is youthful, it reaches maturity, and at some stage it begins to fall apart, just like you and me. Wine aging is a bell-shaped curve. A vintage grows better and better for awhile. Hopefully, when it reaches its peak, it plateaus for a period, then it begins to decline. I'll bore you by repeating that all these judgments are subjective. I remember, for instance, when I was a kid and my father was 35 years old. He was a mountain of a man, about 6' 1", 280 lbs., a railroad laborer who rolled boxcar wheels like you and I would roll a car tire. He generally had neither the energy nor the enthusiasm to play with me after a day of hard work so somehow he always seemed old. I have just turned 50, with children 8, 12, and 13. I imagine that I seem old to them but it's amazing how my perspective has changed. Yes, I tire more quickly and I take longer to recover after I play racquetball with them, but I feel like I'm as productive as I've ever been in my life. Similarly, how a particular vintage is aging has a lot to do with perspective.

Frequently I'm asked, "What's your best wine?" It's the one you like the best. You see, wine is really a very simple subject. I've said it many times and I hope by now it's sinking in. It's so simple that it sometimes scares us, but confidence is the key. Believe in your palate; believe in your judgment. You paid the tab and if you're happy with what you got, that's what counts.

I love the question "How long does a wine keep after you open it?" Around my house the answer is about a half-hour. And, "What do you do with an unfinished bottle?" I don't know; it's not a problem at the Meyer residence. But, realistically, if you don't finish a bottle, recork it and put it in the refrigerator. The colder temperature will slow the chemical reactions and permit less deterioration. Better yet, there are devices that evacuate the air from a bottle's headspace before replacing the cork. Air is usually the culprit causing the break down.

That's not to say, however, that a partial bottle will last forever just because you took the above precaution. Each sample is slowly deteriorating once opened, even if recorked, and should be drunk within a reasonably short time.

How about if you find a bottle with ullage, which is a fancy name for excessive airspace between the cork and the liquid. Obviously it indicates that some wine has been lost, either through leakage or evaporation. I've tasted some wines with considerable headspace in the bottle and found them to be magnificent. On the other hand, a leaky cork might permit air to enter and cause a wine break down. Ullage by itself is neither good nor bad. It does indicate that something unusual has happened. The proof is in the smelling and tasting. I wouldn't pay an exorbitant price for an old bottle of wine that had a lot of headspace. Sediment also doesn't mean the wine will be bad. I'd be perfectly willing to try any bottle that had sediment in it. I would, however, be careful that it was poured very gently or was decanted into another bottle so that my guests or I wouldn't get much sediment in our glasses. If it turned out that the wine was faulty because the sediment was caused by microbiological action, I wouldn't be afraid to return it. But I've tasted many fine vintages which had considerable sediment on the bottom or crustiness on the inside shoulders of the bottle.

How about this one: "Will this wine travel?" I'll guarantee that if you carry it on a plane with you, it'll go wherever your ticket takes you. I can't say with certainty that I've never tasted a wine that was "tired" or "travel sick." I've tasted some poor wines whose defects were blamed on travel. Speaking of travel, I remember once having a "run in" with a wine writer in Houston, Texas. He must've asked me 10 times in the same evening why I did not make half bottles of wine. I guess my real answer was that I thought any two people worth their salt could drink a full bottle. Besides, it costs a lot more money to put wine in half bottles, and it develops much faster in the smaller bottles so it doesn't age nearly as well. Anyway, he wouldn't give up and kept asking me until I finally told him he should start his own damn winery, then he could produce any bottle size he wanted. In his next article he made some sarcastic remarks that suggested I'd been on the road too long that trip and thus was in bad humor. That wasn't the case; I was in bad humor because I was bored and tired of him asking the same silly question over and over. It's much like a wine that you don't like or that you find defective but since it happens to come from one of your favorite producers, you blame it on travel sickness.

I could go on and on. Over the last four years, while I've been working on ideas for this book, I've been noting some of the questions I'm more commonly asked. I hope I've addressed your queries somewhere along the line. But just use your own common sense. Wine is food; it should taste good. It should be fun; you should look forward to it and not be intimidated by it. While there may be lousy wine, there's no such thing as the wrong wine. Maybe you just served it to the wrong people. Maybe you just read the wrong reviewer. So get out there and experiment. Let your palate be your guide and for goodness sakes—enjoy yourself!

*"One last word: never let a
drunkard choose your wine.
You may be sure he knows
nothing about it. It is only
sober people who know
how to drink."*

M. CONSTANTIN-WEYER

12.

Wine Use in the United States

Past, Present, and Future

I have to admit that I'm always a little jealous when I read someone's account of their childhood, how they grew up in a winegrowing or wine-drinking family. Whether or not they liked the fruit of the vine or drank it with their meals, it was always available on the table. Wine was part of their cultural heritage, even though they may not have been conscious of it. People who have come to know and appreciate vino in this fashion never confuse it with beer or spirits. In short, wine is a civilized drink.

When people discovered wine, their quality of life improved. If you've ever enjoyed a meal accompanied by a fine wine, you'll never match its quality with another beverage during your repast—be it liquor, beer, coffee, milk or water. In Europe vino is an integral part of meals. The chapter on "Wine and Your Health" pointed out that evidence overwhelmingly indicates that from a health standpoint, the benefits derived from the moderate use of wine far outweigh the over-publicized problems attributed to it.

So why is wine "under fire" these days? There are groups pushing to see it branded as alcohol—a drug—and, consequently, bad. If you think I'm exaggerating, how about the following: Let's start with the phrase "A drug-free America." It drives me up a wall. Wine is included not only with marijuana, cocaine, and heroin, but also with aspirin, valium, and cortisone. There is no realization that there are differences among drugs and that there is also an important distinction between proper uses of drugs and drug abuse. There are certain drugs which are inherently addictive and other drugs which are not. The "moral entrepreneurs" assign to all drugs identical negative consequences. How, then, are we to perceive doctors and pharmacies? Will they next outlaw the beneficial use of prescription drugs or of wine with meals in many hospitals in this country? How can we possibly, as a nation, include wine under the heading of "drug abuse"? Did you ever hear of a kid squandering his lunch money to buy a bottle of Chardonnay . . . or of a Cabernet lover who has to commit crimes to support his $300 a day habit . . . or of a skid row bum who drinks late-harvest Riesling at $30 per bottle?

Wine use is at a pivotal point in the United States; as the nation becomes more interested in fitness and health, the moderate use of wine can become an integral part of this enlightened lifestyle, as it is in most civilized cultures.

America once understood that wine was a civilized drink not to be confused with hard liquor. Thomas Jefferson sought a clear differentiation between wine and other alcoholic beverages. He recognized that "no nation is drunken where wine is cheap and none sober where the dearness of wine substitutes ardent spirits as the common beverage. Wine brightens the life and thinking of anyone."

Wine is entirely different from booze and beer in its production methods, in its uses, and in its effects. One consumes table wine with food and meals for the flavor and for the effect it has on one's digestion. Hard liquor is consumed for its intoxicating effect. And while beer is part of meals in some countries, its general abuse in the

U.S. occurs when it, like booze, is consumed as an intoxicant. Even at the dawn of Prohibition, most thought it was a foregone conclusion that wine would not be included in that dreadful experiment. Opponents of wine, however, convinced enough politicians of that era that alcohol, no matter what its form, was bad for the country, so total Prohibition thus became law.

Wine as a mealtime beverage presents an entirely different approach to alcohol consumption. I hope the country and the law-makers can recapture the founding fathers' realization that wine is a civilized drink, not to be confused with other beverages containing alcohol and certainly not to be put into the category of abusive drugs. Somehow we must make the public and law-makers understand that, as Paul Claudel observes, a "cocktail is to a glass of wine as rape is to love".

Why is the U.S. so backwards in its attitude toward wine? Why have those of us who produce wine had to deal with the "hung over" and "hung up" attitudes of the government since Prohibition? Wine and the wine industry are certainly not treated with equity. What other industry, in order to sell its products, has to deal with 50 different state laws, and to confront labeling laws devised to harass the industry and make sales more difficult—all under the guise of protecting the consumer? What promontory powers do liquor-control boards have enabling them to correctly determine not only which wines can and cannot be sold in their states, but at what prices? Why has our government become so confused about wine? Why is it that whenever the government cannot balance its budget, among the first places it looks to raise revenues are the wine, liquor and tobacco industries? Is it a crusade against cultural depravity? Those advocating Prohibition or controls on wine under the guise of tolerance are most intolerant of all.

When temperance movements start rolling, they indeed have some positive effects but unfortunate ones also follow. Foremost of the latter is the increase of intolerance. The greatest danger is not that citizens move from more liberal to less liberal attitudes with respect to the availability of alcohol, but rather that the peak enthusiasm of the movement may turn into a moral inquisition. Extreme laws may be enacted creating a backlash which doesn't help anybody and, in the long run, reform becomes distortion.

Do you realize that early in the nineteenth century, the per-capita consumption of alcohol in the United States was three times what it is now? Most was in distilled spirits, seven or eight gallons of ethanol, as compared to the 2.5 we have now. That's a real drinking problem.

Our national experiment with Prohibition didn't work. It was a disaster, creating an artificial desire and exorbitant price for alcohol. Vintners were driven from their trade. Mobsters took control of liquor sales much as they're doing with illegal narcotics today, because of enormous profits to be made. Prohibition caused more crime, more rotgut and more drunks than could have ever been expected without it.

Historically in America, the more people affected and the more severe the laws concerning alcohol, the more profound has been their ineffectiveness. The reason is that Americans are very diverse culturally, heterogeneous, with widely different customs and norms concerning alcoholic consumption or abstinence. Moreover, Americans don't like being told what they can or cannot do.

"God in his goodness sent the grape to
cheer both great and small. Little fools
will drink too much and great fools
none at all."
ANONYMOUS

Today's temperance movement is focused on drunk driving, which everyone agrees is an evil. A second impulse toward temperance today is the growth of a health movement, but this could also favor wine, if it is recognized as a dignified drink to be used in moderation with food and not bunched with beer and hard liquor. The foundation of the temperance movement today is made up of grass-roots organizations led by ordinary citizens like Mothers Against Drunk Driving (M.A.D.D.) and Students Against Drunk Driving (S.A.D.D.). This is the public saying that we have to take action in face of a difficult situation, namely driving while intoxicated. While I have the greatest empathy for such rational groups, let's not let emotion muddle the facts.

Years ago a report sponsored by the Department of Police Administration of Indiana University which led to the acceptance of certain blood alcohol levels causing driving impairment revealed that "those who drank wine in preference to other alcoholic beverages contributed almost nothing to the number of those with blood alcohol levels over .05 percent."

A more recent study by the Department of Justice of drunk drivers serving jail terms indicated only 2 percent had drunk only wine before their arrest; 54 percent had consumed only beer, 28 percent had drunk only liquor, and 21 percent had mixed more than one type of alcoholic beverage. So let's examine the facts clearly. Prohibiting wine, or making it more difficult to obtain, or putting additional excise taxes on it, will do almost nothing to cure the drunk driving problem even though some neo-prohibitionist groups would like you to believe otherwise.

Here are some other smokescreens put forward in an attempt to discredit wine. Follow the logic closely or you'll miss the slight of hand. Have you ever heard of the "salad bar syndrome"? One of these neo-prohibitionist organizations has brought to the attention of the government the news that a tiny percentage of the population, which is highly allergic to sulfur dioxide, has experienced sulfite poisoning from salad bars. The false conclusion is that since there are also sulfites in wine, the wine industry should thus be required to put a warning label on its bottles. Despite the fact that some salad bars have been known to use sulfur dioxide in concentrations of more than 1,000 parts per million, the wine industry is compelled by the government to make a sulfite statement on the label if a product contains more than 10 parts per million sulfite! The accompanying irony is that the government has imposed this ruling, even though there is no approved chemical analysis for measuring sulfites in wine at this concentration. Could it be that salads are much more harmful for us than wine?

Then there's the charge that urethane, a natural ingredient that results from yeast fermentation in wine, is carcenogenic. It turns out that a common loaf of bread contains urethane and one would have to drink approximately 200 bottles of wine per day to cause any cancerous effect. You could drown in this much wine long before developing cancer. Peanut butter, bread, diet cola, mushrooms, basil, lettuce, parsley, radishes, corn, tap water, and swimming-pool water have all been shown to have detectable amounts of carcinogens. If we pursue this kind of sophistic reasoning, we will have warning signs at grocery store entrances stating that most everything inside is harmful to your health.

Imagine how amazed a Frenchman or an Italian would be to hear someone say wine is carcenogenic. He drinks 10 times as much as an average American, chain smokes lousy tobacco, and doesn't see nearly the incidence of cancer as in the U.S.

We cannot ignore the fact that the federal government is a "moral entrepreneur." Bureaucratic organizations have a tendency to perpetuate themselves. Reflect on how many government agencies have ever put themselves out of business; their tendency, rather, is to escalate our problems in order to match their similarly-behaving budgets. When you hear of states outlawing happy hours and of the federal government requiring states to increase the drinking age lest they lose funds for federal highway taxes, you wonder how far the campaign can proceed. The latter is a very interesting form of tax-supported blackmail. Finally, all levels of government need lots of money since they cannot or will not balance their budgets. Isn't the argument by neo-prohibitionist groups—that taxes should be increased on all products containing alcohol—very attractive to politicians? I like Will Rogers' comment in his book *The Cowboy Philosopher on Prohibition*: "Congress voted dry but drinks wet"!

A goal for the year 2,000 might well be the attainment of a healthy national atmosphere, one which will be conducive for those who can and will drink moderately, allowing them to do so without guilt or fear. Those who choose to abstain can enjoy the same degree of freedom; those who, for whatever reason develop drinking problems, can recognize them at the earliest possible stage and seek appropriate help.

Such an atmosphere would inevitably result in the minimalization of all alcohol-related problems. These problems are now and have been for some years decreasing, as legitimate statistics indicate. Predictably, they'll continue in general to decrease for some time to come. If these reductions are accompanied by sound, constructive and

145

proven-positive educational approaches, we have an excellent chance to ensure their permanence. If, on the other hand, we misguidedly impose severe legal restrictions, we'll simply be sowing the seeds for an increase in alcohol problems for today's children and for future generations.

In wine-drinking and wine-producing countries, such as Italy, Greece, Portugal, and Spain, where we find that alcoholism is not a national problem, we also find that drunkeness is not acceptable or considered funny. We find, too, that wine is sold in food stores next to food, since it is to be consumed with food. A study published in 1953 in the *Quarterly Journal of Studies on Alcohol* first noted that high per-capita wine consumption and low rates of alcohol abuse are norms in these countries. In Russia, where vodka is the principal drink, alcoholism is an immense problem. In fact, the Communist government has been trying for years to develop a wine industry and to convert its people to drinking vino in order to reduce alcoholism.

Vintners must take responsibility for some of the attitudes that we encounter about wine. Though our industry's advertising code has been responsible, our advertising leaves something to be desired. One would think that you can't enjoy wine unless you are sitting at a gourmet, black-tie dinner with music provided by a string quartet. We haven't conveyed the message that wine adds to the good life, makes a good meal even better, and can be enjoyed with a hamburger at a picnic. We, as an industry, have hurt wine by what we've said and how we've said it. We need to adopt the approach of Alan Richman who said, "Anyone introducing a beginner to wine should be aware that the greatest danger is not overindulgence in wine, but overindulgence in wine talk. After listening to a detailed explanation of a wine label, the beginner will feel that the wine isn't worth drinking if he has to associate with people who drink it."

In my opinion, we've too many gurus and snobs connected with the wine business, and they've intimidated more potential wine drinkers than they've won over. In fact, the ultimate abuse occurs in the wine business when some of these people begin to believe the myths which they have used to infect the minds of an unsuspecting public.

Let's get back to basics. When I started this book, I surveyed friends in the wine business to see which topics they felt should be covered. The most popular, overriding theme that came back was:

"Tell people to trust their own palates."

"Tell people not to be initmidated by the gurus, snobs and, yes, even the wine producer."

"Tell people if they enjoy a wine, drink it and don't be concerned about whether or not they can articulate why they like it."

Wine is like music—you may not know what is good, but you know what you like! It all gets back to PLAIN TALK ABOUT FINE WINE.

If God forbade drinking, would He
have made wine so good?
CARDINAL RICHELIEU

AFTERWORD

From the porch of Justin and Bonny's house near Oakville, I have gazed west toward the rainy side of Napa Valley, where quiet hills are so darkly forested with conifers that they blacken as the sun lowers. Viewed from the house's deck, to the east across a verdant vineyard, other mountains loom, drier with dark slashes of trees defining their creases and mounds. Those varied vistas are startling, but there is a greater contrast in Justin's life . . .

From the front porch of the house in Baskerfield where the kid we then called Raymie Meyer was raised I many times viewed the railroad switching yard across the street, heard the explosive coupling of cars, the snorting exertion of engines. In back, behind a rickety garage, was an unpaved alley where children played and chattered in two languages.

The distance between those two sites—three hundred miles by airplane—is greater when opportunity, hard work, and professional achievement are factored in. And that distance, traveled by a bright, blue-collar kid from the tough side of town, defines a realization of the American dream.

In 1950, when we were junior high school students, I met the towheaded athlete who would become Justin Meyer. As years went by, I was there when his knee was destroyed in a football collision, there when he climbed onstage and sang an unlikely duet with Fats Domino, there when he walked out of that house to begin the circuitous, unexpected odyssey that has led to Oakville.

We've been pals for nearly forty years and the characteristic I most value in our friendship is that, as success and honors have accumulated in Justin's life, his directness and spontaneity have not faltered. You really can expect plain talk from him. You know where he stands because he knows. His approach to life is like his approach to fine wine, straight-forward but not simplistic.

True, his svelte figure now resembles a linebacker's rather than a halfback's; yes, his hairline has departed for Chihuahua. But I can never talk to Justin without encountering Raymie, and I like them both. He makes a great cabernet, too.

GERALD HASLAM
Penngrove, California